CATALYSTS AND WATCHDOGS

B.C.'s Men of God: 1836-1871

JOAN WEIR

Sono Nis Press 1995
VICTORIA, BRITISH COLUMBIA, CANADA

Canadian Cataloguing in Publication Data

Weir, Joan, 1928-
  Catalysts and watchdogs

  Includes bibliographical references and index.
  ISBN 1-55039-055-4

  1. Missions—British Columbia—History—1849-1871. 2.
Church and state—British Columbia—History—19th century. 3.
Indians of North America—British Columbia—Missions. I.
Title.
BV2815.B7W44 1994   266′009711′09034   C94-910616-X

This book was published with the assistance of the
Canada Council Block Grant Program.

Financially assisted by the Government of British Columbia
through the B.C. Heritage Trust.

Published by
SONO NIS PRESS
1745 Blanshard Street
Victoria, British Columbia
Canada v8w 2j8

Printed and bound in Canada by
MORRISS PRINTING COMPANY LTD.
Victoria, British Columbia

This book is dedicated with love and gratitude in memory of my father:

Archbishop L. Ralph Sherman

Archbishop of Rupert's Land 1943-1952
Bishop of Calgary 1927-1943

I am not afraid of poverty or of labour, but I am afraid of doing less than my all, or of offering to God that which costs me as little as possible.

THE REVEREND JAMES REYNARD

Barkerville, 1865

CONTENTS

Photos follow page 48

Chapter 1

BEGINNINGS

H ISTORY, like the people who shape it, is the sum total of its composite parts. Take away any of those parts—or put them into different combinations—and the end result might be different.

It is interesting to consider the diffuse and varied contribution made by the early Men of God to the development of the province of British Columbia. They first arrived in the far west in the mid-1830s. How important was their presence during the three-and-a-half decades that followed leading up to British Columbia's entry into Confederation? Without the Men of God might history have been different?

During the 1840s and 1850s and particularly during the vital decade from 1860 to 1870 this area was not only uncivilized, it was also isolated. It was effectively screened from any supervisory eyes in eastern Canada by 3,000 miles of wilderness and by a ridge of impassable mountains. It was effectively screened from supervisory eyes in Britain by the same wilderness, the same mountains and by an additional 3,000 miles of ocean. As a result, during the years when direction or criticism from experienced leaders in central Canada or Britain would have been valuable to help shape and mold what was soon to become Canada's newest province, that advice was either not forthcoming, or took so long to reach its destination that it was no longer of much practical value. Far-west policy-makers, politicians, legal authorities and business entrepreneurs were potentially free to do almost as they pleased.

Might history have been any different if the Men of God had not been here exerting their influence on moral, political and social issues?

How important was their questioning, arguing, opposing, supporting and suggesting?

Admittedly, their influence was not always effective; perhaps their intervention was not always beneficial. Unquestionably, there are times when they can be faulted for inexperience, over-zealousness and ineffectiveness. But there were times when the Men of God provided both expertise and leadership. There were times when they served as the only available brake, counter-balance, mentor or sounding-board.

†

The first Man of God to come to the Canadian far west was brought in by the Hudson's Bay Company. He was Herbert Beaver, brought west in 1836 to be the Company chaplain at Fort Vancouver.

The intention was that Beaver would provide church services for fort personnel, conduct school classes for the fort children, and by his presence smooth away some of the rough edges of frontier life.

The reality was far different.

†

As early as 1680, just ten years after the granting of its charter, the Hudson's Bay Company had first publicly expressed its intention of promoting some sort of religious observance in all its western trading posts.

"Wee [*sic*] do strictly enjoin you to have public prayers and reading of the Scriptures . . . wheresoever you shall be resident," the Governor and Committee in London instructed John Nixon, Governor of Rupert's Land, "that wee who profess to be Christians may not appear more barbarous than the poor Heathens themselves."[1]

This injunction was not ignored. Subsequent journals show that some sort of Sunday observance became standard practice at most of the Hudson's Bay Company trading posts. But until well into the nineteenth century these services were conducted by fort personnel, not by ordained clergymen. It wasn't until 1819 that the first actual clergyman, the Reverend John West, was installed as Company chaplain at Fort Red River, in the area that was to become Manitoba. Soon other clerics were appointed. And when in 1826 following his tour of the Columbia district, Governor George Simpson reported to the Governor and Committee in London that he did "not know any part of North America where the Natives could be civilized and instructed in morality and Religion at such a moderate expense,"[2] the sending of a clergyman to one of the new western Canadian Hudson's Bay posts seemed imminent.

In actuality, however, it was ten more years before this happened. Historian Hollis Slater suggests that Simpson himself may have been responsible. Although he had initiated the idea of sending a clergyman west, he had accompanied that suggestion with dire warnings.

> The missionary [must] be cool and temperate in his habits and of a mild conciliatory disposition . . . not too much disposed to find fault with any little laxity of Morals he may discover . . . He ought to understand in the outset that nearly all the Gentlemen and Servants have families, although Marriage ceremonies are unknown . . . It would be all in vain to attempt breaking through this uncivilized custom. . . . So much depends on the character and disposition of the Missionary that the Society could not be too particular.[3]

As a result of Simpson's warning, the Governor and Committee in London proceeded slowly. In 1830 they began tentative discussions with two potential candidates for the post of chaplain at Fort Vancouver, but when both declined, each using his wife's fears of the seven-month sea voyage around Cape Horn as an excuse, the Company did no urging. Then Simpson himself must have decided that it was only a question of time before someone arrived in his western territory and began organizing religious services and preaching religion. If it wasn't a man sent out by the Hudson's Bay officials in London, then it would be one of the aggressive American missionaries who were already showing signs of wanting to push northward. He must have decided that the lesser of two evils would be to personally select the man he would have to deal with. Accordingly, when he was in England in 1835 he selected Herbert Beaver, B.A., to be the first Hudson's Bay chaplain west of the Rockies.

A worse choice is hard to imagine. If Simpson did not soon regret his choice, everyone at Fort Vancouver did. It took Beaver seven months of seasickness and unpalatable rations to round the Cape and take over his new position at Fort Vancouver. It took him just seven weeks after his arrival to foment sufficient friction and controversy to threaten the very structure of fur-trade society that sustained Fort Vancouver. A considerable accomplishment for someone historian W. H. Gray describes as "a man below medium height, with a feminine voice, large pretensions to oratory, a poor delivery and no energy."[4]

Admittedly, his new home was not exactly modern for it was only 1836, but it was far from barbaric. In fact, compared with many Hudson's Bay posts it was moderately comfortable. However, Beaver didn't think so. Shortly after his arrival he sent a letter back to the headquarters of the Hudson's Bay Company in London railing, "I feel defiled and polluted. There is not an individual about the establishment with whom I feel I can associate. The Governor is uncivil, the clerks are bores, the women are savages."[5]

After eight weeks he applied to go home, then reconsidered and stayed for two years. But during that two years he and his wife, whom the post personnel referred to as Haughty Jane, came to figurative blows with everyone they met, and to literal blows with Beaver's boss, Chief Factor John McLoughlin. In November 1838, shortly before Beaver left, the two men actually attacked each other physically on the hard-packed dust of the fort compound.[6]

The Hudson's Bay Company waited ten years after Beaver's departure before selecting a successor, but the length of their deliberations did not ensure any more wisdom in their choice. Nor did their decision this time to appoint a schoolteacher, not an ordained clergyman.

The new chaplain, Robert John Staines, arrived early in 1849. His destination was Victoria, which was even less civilized than Fort Vancouver. If Beaver had been dismayed, Staines was doubly so. The years of his tenure were marked by even greater controversy than Beaver's had been, not only on moral and doctrinal issues, but with legal and political implications as well. After barely four years at Fort Victoria, Staines left in anger in 1853.

Two years later the Hudson's Bay brought in another Man of God to be their third and last far-west chaplain. The man they selected this time was Edward Cridge, an experienced and vocal Church of England clergyman who was as outspoken as his two predecessors had been.

Cridge was curate-in-charge of a parish in Stratford, London, when in the summer of 1854 he learned from the vicar of a neighbouring parish that the Hudson's Bay Company was looking for a chaplain for Fort Victoria.

> The vicar of West Ham thought that if I applied I might very likely obtain it. . . . I consented to become a candidate . . . led to this decision by the consideration that God might perhaps by this means be answering my prayers and petitions.[7]

Interviews with the Hudson's Bay Company followed, and Cridge was offered the appointment on the condition that he sail immediately.

At first he hesitated, for he was engaged to be married and the wedding plans had not yet been made. However, he must have been eager to go, for on Thursday September 14th, just weeks after his interview with the Hudson's Bay Company, he and his fiancée, Mary Winnell, were married at the West Ham Parish Church and sailed the following Wednesday for Canada. Twenty-seven weeks later on April 1st 1855 they reached Victoria.

Six years earlier, Staines, on his arrival in Victoria, had ranted about the barbaric conditions that existed. Cridge's reaction was significantly different. Finding himself and his wife billeted in the Fort until their parsonage was ready, Cridge commented on the "large and airy rooms" which he said were "a pleasant change from the cramped quarters of the ship." As for the city of Victoria, he wrote:

> I know not what the population of Victoria might be, though I think two hundred would be the outside; the population of the whole Island being about six hundred. You could count the houses on each side of the four principal streets, Government, Fort, Yates, Johnson, on the fingers of one hand.[8]

From the moment of his arrival in the Canadian far west Cridge's influence was significant, perhaps because his area of involvement was more diffuse than had been either Beaver's or Staines's — perhaps because he stayed a great deal longer — perhaps because he arrived at a crucial point in far-west history — also perhaps because of his own personality. Not only was he strong-minded and self-confident, he was also courageous and outspoken. Before he was through he broke from the established church, founded a new church of his own which he called the Reformed Episcopal Church of the Pacific Coast, and declared himself bishop.

By the time Cridge arrived in Victoria, however, Hudson's Bay chaplains were no longer the only ones in the area organizing church services and preaching religion. Other theologically trained missionaries had moved westward. The first to come had been Roman Catholic Fathers Modeste Demers and François Blanchet. Originally sent west from Quebec in 1838, charged with the task of establishing missions in the Cowlitz Valley north of the Columbia River, Demers and Blanchet left the Cowlitz Valley early in the 1840s and moved to the more densely populated area of Victoria. In 1849 they were joined by a third Roman Catholic missionary, Father Lempfrit.

In 1851 Father Modeste Demers was consecrated Roman Catholic Bishop of Victoria. No longer was he responsible just for the spiritual welfare of his own parishioners. Now, as bishop of this vast area he was charged with the responsibility of teaching the Roman Catholic faith to all its residents. Accordingly, in 1858 he made a trip back to Quebec to recruit people to help him, bringing back with him at that time Father Rondeault, Father Donkele, and four Sisters of St. Anne whose job it was to start a Roman Catholic school.

Then, the following year the leisured pace of missionary enterprise in Canada's far west changed dramatically. In November 1859, in London's famed Mansion House, the Columbia Mission Society was founded. The Society took as its mandate the challenge of "establishing the Christian church throughout the entire Canadian region west of the Rocky Mountains."

Within three months the first group of Columbia Mission clerics was on board ship making their way westward—Bishop George Hills, the Rev. R. J. Dundas, the Rev. John Sheepshanks, the Rev. Alexander C. Garrett, the Rev. R. L. Lowe, the Rev. Christopher Knipe, and the Rev. Lunden Brown. More were to follow. The influx of Men of God into the western wilderness had begun in earnest.

†

The list of founding members at the inaugural meeting of the Columbia Mission Society reads like a page from DeBrett's Peerage. The chairman was the Right Honourable William Cubitt, Lord Mayor of London. Members in attendance included the Right Reverend Lord Bishops of London, Oxford, Perth, and British Columbia; the Dean and the Vicar of St. Paul's Cathedral; the Right Honorable Sir G. Grey, Baronet, Governor of the Cape; Sir Harry Verny, Baronet; members of parliament Arthur Kinnaird, A. Cubitt, Wm. Tite, Danby Seymour, and T. Christie; and more than a score of professional dignitaries and influential men of business. Members unable to attend in person included the Archbishop of Canterbury, His Grace the Duke of Newcastle (attending a meeting of the cabinet), Sir William Page Wood, the Bishop of Asaph, and the Honourable Robert Hanbury, M.P.

According to the Lord Mayor of London's opening speech, spreading the word of God in this most westerly section of the Canadian wilderness was ". . . a solemn duty. The finger of Providence may be perceived . . . the Anglo-Saxon races have had an opportunity given them of extending themselves yet more widely."[9]

It is unfortunate that the Columbia Mission did not recognize the uniqueness of the Canadian far west. Had they done so the task of these early missionaries might have been simplified. Instead the concern of the Columbia Mission was to establish in the Canadian wilderness a church that duplicated in every way the structured, ritualistic church in England. Moreover, the men to be chosen to establish this church were to be well-educated, upper-class English clerics steeped in traditional church doctrine, with degrees from Oxford or Cambridge in Latin, Greek and literature.

"I thank God that he has enabled us to send out the Church in the way in which we have it at home, in its perfectness and completeness," stated the Bishop of Oxford at this founding meeting.

"May we be able to plant there no meagre seedling of our beloved Church, but ... its full institutions ... our scriptural formularies ... our system of Church government," agreed the newly appointed Bishop of British Columbia.[10]

The problem was that neither man, nor indeed any member at that founding meeting, realized the situation that existed in the area they were planning to Christianize. They assumed that this new area west of the Rockies would be populated largely by Englishmen, and that these resident Englishmen would prepare for and welcome the missionaries. This was not the case. Apart from the several thousand gold-seekers who were arriving at precisely the same time as these first missionaries, the majority of residents of this vast area were Indians. They had neither invited, nor were they expecting the missionaries. As a result the Men of God arrived to find no house ready for them, no building in which to hold services, and often no stipend.

One of the greatest difficulties facing the missionaries was finding a way to teach, advise and convert people who did not speak the same language, particularly when those people were nomadic and moved with the game and the seasons. Any sort of a cumulative learning pattern was impossible. To further complicate things, apart from the limited "fur-trade Chinook" that was used by those actively involved in the fur trade, there was no common First Nations language. More than thirty local dialects were spoken in the area.

Paradoxically, the magnitude of the problems facing the missionaries gradually worked towards the solution. As news of the difficulties facing the western missionaries filtered back to England, more and more upper-class, Oxford- or Cambridge-educated clerics decided against volunteering for foreign duty. They elected instead to remain in their established parishes. The church found itself forced to train a new class of missionary volunteer—men from working-class homes and labouring backgrounds, who ironically were better fitted to succeed in this western region than their upper-class compatriots. Having already learned to improvise and invent in order to survive, these men arrived in the far west better able to find ways to surmount these difficulties of language and mobility.

In 1859, however, the reality of the situation in far-west Canada was still unknown. The concern of the Columbia Mission was to send the "best" man in England to be bishop of this new region, supported by the "best" group of missionaries. "Best" meant upper-class parentage and Oxford or Cambridge education.

One wonders to what extent the personality of these supposedly "best" clerics—their tenacity, their biases, their shortcomings—can be held responsible for much of the controversy and many of the problems that marked the church's first years in the area.

But the Columbia Mission thought they were acting in the best interests of the church and of the far-west Canadian frontier when they selected the men they did. They chose men whom they firmly believed in, starting with George Hills.

Until selected to be bishop of this new Diocese of British Columbia on Canada's far-west frontier, Hills had been rector of the most prominent upper-class parish in Yarmouth. He was energetic, intellectual, angular and humourless. He attracted notice the moment he arrived. As he was being conducted on horseback to visit his new diocese the clerics accompanying him wiled away the hours by singing and whistling. Hills insisted they stop. Henceforth, he stated, there was to be neither singing nor whistling in his presence. It did not show sufficient respect for his ecclesiastical office.[11]

Hills's name had been put before the Columbia Mission as the best man to be bishop of this new diocese by Baroness Angela Burdett-Coutts. Her recommendation was accepted because it was her private bequest of fifteen thousand pounds that was financing the venture. Some years later Burdett-Coutts and Hills found themselves in open conflict, but at the outset the Baroness considered the upper-class, high-minded Hills the perfect ambassador to carry the English church into the Canadian wilderness.

It seemed Hills shared her belief. During the months'-long sea voyage to Canada most of the passengers, including the ship's surgeon, fell seriously ill with yellow fever. Hills was one of the few who did not. One of his journal entries includes the comment that this was proof indeed of the importance of his person in the eyes of God.

To assist him in this new life in the Canadian wilderness Hills brought with him his uniformed, London-trained manservant, William. One of William's duties was to accompany his master on his numerous month-long horseback journeys around the diocese. Such journeys took them through thick underbrush, hordes of mosquitoes, and over often impassable terrain, and according to John Sheepshanks who wrote a history of Hills's early years as bishop, "the faithful William did not much relish the rough work of missionary travel."[12] Perhaps it is not surprising that before many months had passed there was no further mention of the faithful William in Hills's daily Journal entries.

From the outset Hills found his new life far different from what he had been used to and far different from what he had expected. His journal entry just two or three days after arriving in Victoria comments on "the discomforts . . . the difficulty in getting servants . . . of having to labour with one's own hands."[13] His first meeting with the governor of the colony, Sir James Douglas, was evidently both a shock and a disappointment, but perhaps it reflects more markedly on Hills than on Douglas. Writing about it in his journal, Hills castigates the Governor for being uncivil and boorish, then explains it away with the comment, "He [Douglas] does not know the tone of a high-minded gentleman . . . owing to the fact that he has never lived in England."

The initial group of clerics recruited at the same time as Hills—John Sheepshanks, Christopher Knipe, Lunden Brown, Alexander Garrett, R. J. Dundas, R. L. Lowe—found, like their bishop, that life on the far-west frontier was difficult. This is not surprising. Not only were the missionaries ignored by the Indian population who spoke no English and so could not communicate with them, but they could not even be sure of a welcome from some of the fur-trade personnel, for in the eyes of many fur-trade people the church posed a major threat to the survival of fur-trade society.

In justification, this fear was not unfounded. The actions of Hudson's Bay chaplains Beaver and Staines had seemed deliberately designed to strike at the hierarchical structure on which fur-trade society was based.

Fur-trade society depended on strict segregation of its classes. At the bottom were the First Nations people who brought in the skins. They spoke their own native dialects and followed their own religion. In the middle were the voyageurs, the transporters. They were almost exclusively French-speaking and followed the Roman Catholic religion. At the top were the Hudson's Bay Company traders and officials. This group included a sizable minority of Roman Catholics but the majority were Protestant, and all spoke English.

The strength of this hierarchy lay in the rigidly preserved separation of the sections. Beaver and Staines and many of the missionaries who followed worked constantly to break through these separating barriers.

Another essential girder supporting fur-trade society was the acceptance of common-law marriages. Not only did this provide stability in the lives of Company officials and fort personnel, but the First Nations "wives" provided an essential communication link between the officials at the top and the trappers at the bottom. The chaplains and missionaries, however, seemed obsessed with the need to stamp out common-law marriages.

A third factor essential to the preservation of fur-trade society was the nomadic life-style of the First Nations people. The fur trade could only survive if the First Nations trappers followed the game and moved with the seasons. Here again the missionaries worked in opposition. Admittedly their reason for this was sound in that they wanted the First Nations people to settle down so the church could minister to them and educate their children, but their action was one more factor contributing to the disintegration of fur-trade society.

No wonder many fur-trade officials and fort personnel eyed with misgivings the steadily growing numbers of missionaries coming into the region. No wonder many of the early missionaries felt ignored and unwelcome. It is to their credit and to the province's benefit that they stayed. Overall, the accomplishments of the Men of God far outweigh their failures. They provided religious services in every area of this western province. They established the first schools for white pupils and for First Nations children. They brought order and often renewed hope to the residents of the gold-fields. They had the courage to speak out when influential politicians or law officers were in danger of overstepping their authority. They mediated the first native land claim disputes.

Admittedly they made mistakes, principally in their residential school program for native children, but they also had successes, and their contribution to the formation of the province of British Columbia is undeniable.

Chapter 2

RIVALRY AND PREJUDICE

THE PROBLEM of trying to preach religion to a people who understood no English and no French was not the only factor hampering the efforts of the early Roman Catholic and Protestant missionaries. They were also hampered by their conviction that they must convert the native people not only to Christianity, but also to a lifestyle and value system that matched the missionaries' own.

They were hampered by a third problem as well. This was the rivalry and intolerance that existed between the missionaries of the different church denominations, as each group tried to outdo the others in influence and numbers of converts.

Roman Catholic/Anglican rivalry was apparent from the outset. Bishop George Hills and his fellow Anglican clerics had not even been recruited, and the Columbia Mission Society was not yet founded when Oblate Father Louis D'herbomez (later to become Bishop of the Vicariate of Melitopolis) wrote to Bishop de Mazenod pleading to be allowed to establish Roman Catholic missions in mainland British Columbia. The letter was dated April 6, 1859 and ended, "Time is pressing. The English Church have already an Episcopal See; their ministers are travelling in all directions and know as well as we do how to choose the best places for the success of their purpose."[14]

It is possible that this letter may have been partially motivated by D'herbomez's determination to establish his Oblates in mainland British Columbia independent from Demers's Catholic Diocese of Victoria, but nonetheless it reflects a genuine fear of any uncontrolled spread of Anglicanism.

Hills was no less outspoken in his fear of the uncontrolled spread of Roman Catholicism. Consistently in his journal and in his correspondence he urged the importance of preventing the expansion of the Roman Catholic Church's influence. This was the prime motive behind his urgency in establishing the Boys' Collegiate School in Victoria within a year of his own arrival, and Angela College for Girls shortly afterward.

Personal rivalry between the two Victoria bishops, Hills and Demers, started within days of their meeting. In a journal entry dated January 1860 Hills accused Roman Catholic Bishop Demers, whom he described as "a coarse looking but good-natured man," of cutting off his milk supply. Demers retaliated by accusing Hills of building a fence which "blocked his way to the cemetery." Hills may subsequently have regretted initiating the confrontation, for Demers took him to court over the cemetery fence and won.

It wasn't only the Roman Catholics and the Anglicans who were guilty of such rivalry. In 1847, Presbyterian Missionary Henry Spalding accused the Roman Catholics of having incited the infamous Whitman Massacre when Dr. Marcus Whitman, his wife Narcissa, and fourteen others were killed by Indians at the Presbyterian mission in Washington. In retaliation the Roman Catholic missionaries told the Indians not to receive the Presbyterian clerics, for "they tell lies."

A few years later David Sallosalton, a young native catechist in the Port Simpson area working with Wesleyan missionary Thomas Crosby, arrived to take a service soaking wet and half frozen. He claimed he had been forced to swim the river in near freezing temperatures because rival missionaries were waiting at his usual fording spot to prevent his crossing.

In this case the action of the rival missionaries was probably a reaction to Sallosalton's popularity, for he had a huge following not only with the native people but with non-natives as well. He first started training under Thomas Crosby in 1865 when he was 12 years old. When he died just seven years later at the age of nineteen, probably of tuberculosis, he was known throughout the area for what was referred to as his "Whistle Boat Sermon." Delivered in broken English, it ended:

> My dear white friends. . . . It is all same as steamboat on this river. [Fraser] When she going to start she whistle one whistle, then she whistle another, and if you don't get your things very quick and run, she whistle third last time and go off and leave you behind. You very sorry because you too late. Jesus like that. He whistle, He call, He whistle and whistle. . . .
>
> Now my white friends, you hurry up or you be too late. . . . Come on board quick. This is very good ship. Room for all.[15]

This sermon alone is credited with large numbers of conversions.

At that time conversions were the only yardstick for measuring the success of a missionary's efforts. Not only did impressive numbers of conversions give a specific denomination status in the eyes of the local people, but it also guaranteed the missionaries of that denomination continued financial support from their parent church. As a result, each group pushed hard to outdo the other.

As early as 1841 Simpson warned of the danger. In a letter to London, he wrote, "the country is studded with missions." He went on to list twelve different missionary stations within one small area with a combined total of twenty-three active missionaries.[16]

Each year after 1841 the number of missionaries increased. So did each denomination's enthusiasm for converts. Had anyone taken the trouble to add up the numbers, a wildly distorted picture of population figures must have emerged, for the native population had no wish to insult any of the visiting missionaries and were quite willing to be baptised by the Anglicans one day, the Roman Catholics the next, and by the Methodists or Baptists the third.

In an attempt to minimize such competition, "agreements" were sometimes made between the various denominations. For example, the New England Company of the Anglican Church (The Society for the Propagation of the Gospel Amongst the Heathen in New England and Adjoining Colonies) decided to try to gain a foothold on Kuper Island, only to find that the Roman Catholic Church was already firmly established there. Accordingly it was agreed that if the Anglicans would leave Kuper Island alone, they could have the Lytton area instead. It was this "agreement" that made possible the establishment of St. George's Residential School at Lytton, and All Hallows Residential School near Yale.

Another "agreement" was made in the Cowichan/Salt Spring Island area. The first church services there were conducted by the Methodist missionaries—first by Sutherland, then by Ebenezer Robson. It was expected that a Methodist church would be built there, but large numbers of Baptists began moving in. Rather than having two rival churches competing for supporters in one small area, it was privately agreed that the Methodists would move out and give the Baptists free rein in the Cowichan Valley, in return for which the Methodists would be given no competition in the Duncan area.

Such agreements were not the only indication that a spirit of ecumenism would some day emerge. There were other hopeful signs. For example, when Missionary Arthur Browning built his Methodist church in New Westminster, the names of the financial contributors on his subscription list included "Catholics, Jews and Confucians, but only one Methodist."[17]

The first non-Catholic church hall in the Cowichan Valley, built by Anglican missionary Alexander C. Garrett, had the same kind of inter-denominational support. Historian Ellen Mackay suggests that when this church hall was built in 1863 at Somenos Lake, "not just the Anglicans worked and contributed. The builders and users of this church hall were *all* the residents, irrespective of denomination."[18]

But despite these indications that a spirit of ecumenism would some day emerge, during the early years in Canada's far west interdenominational co-operation was not common. Religious intolerance was much more likely to be evinced, and not just by the missionaries of the various churches. Fur-trade personnel were equally guilty.

The potential for confrontation and dissatisfaction was built into the very heart of fur-trade society. The top level of the hierarchy who made the rules and meted out the decisions was predominantly Protestant. The middle level who did the work and took the orders was predominantly Roman Catholic. The bottom level, the First Nations trappers, were pawns for both groups as the missionaries of all denominations sought to win financial support at home by reporting impressive numbers of converts.

Had the top level of the hierarchy practiced religious tolerance a great many problems might have been avoided, but it was not an era of religious tolerance. It was an era of religious competition.

The onset of trouble can not be blamed on the arrival of the mission-aries. It began long before, perhaps from the moment of the merger between the Hudson's Bay Company and the Nor'Westers in 1821. From that moment on the potential for trouble was present under the surface. But though the missionaries cannot be held responsible for the escalation of religious intolerance, Hudson's Bay chaplains Beaver and Staines cer-tainly fanned the embers. All that was needed was a spark to ignite them, and that spark was provided by Hudson's Bay Governor George Simpson.

A young, raw-mannered trader, the out-of-wedlock son of lower-class English parents, Simpson was ill educated, abrasive and insensitive to the point of cruelty, yet he rose with surprising swiftness to a position of authority. With the merger of the two fur-trade companies in 1821, Simpson was appointed governor of the expanded Northern Department in Rupert's Land. Immediately he set about reconstructing the fur trade in his district, area by area.

By 1824 he had reorganized to his satisfaction all but the far-west region of Columbia and was impatient to tackle this. Accordingly, in 1824 he made his first trip to the far west. Four years later in July, 1828, now governor of both the Northern and Southern Departments of the Hudson's Bay fur trade, Simpson set out on his second trip to the far west.

Ironically, the failings Simpson most objected to in others were shortcomings he failed to recognize in himself. Tolerance on any level — racial, religious or social — was missing from his makeup. With his meteoric rise to power, his callous disregard for any views other than his own grew steadily more pronounced.

On his second trip west in 1828 he had no difficulty allowing all the activities of his party to stop each evening while his personal piper, Colin Fraser, leisurely serenaded him with Scottish music. He found time each morning for his party to stand idle while the personnel at each fort he visited sent him on his way with three rousing cheers and a lengthy, formally conducted seven-gun salute, but he could not find the time to stop either to rest his horses or to water them.[19] As a result more than two and a half dozen prime animals died unnecessarily on the trek.

This callous insensitivity was not restricted to animals. Letters to his mentor and patron Andrew Colville during his early years of service with the Company revealed the depth and intensity of Simpson's prejudice. He admitted frankly that he opposed establishing schools for native children because "an enlightened Indian is good for nothing."[20] He went on to say that he regretted the Company's decision to restrict the provision of alcohol to the Indians, for "it is a great [work] stimulus."[21]

The Hudson's Bay Company subsequently forced Simpson to moderate his views on both these matters by making it clear to him that such views ran counter to both Company and public opinion. But though this may have caused him to guard his tongue, it did not lessen the prejudice he continued to demonstrate towards the native people, the half-breed offspring of fur-trade marriages, and the Roman Catholic Church.

It was inevitable, therefore, that he would clash with Dr. John McLoughlin, Hudson's Bay Chief Factor at Fort Vancouver, for McLoughlin was a Roman Catholic, happily living *à la façon du pays* with an Indian woman, and their half-breed son, John Junior.

John McLoughlin Senior had long known, of course, of Simpson's prejudice against him. When his son, John, had first reached employable age McLoughlin had written to his friend, explorer Simon Fraser, for advice.

Fraser's reply was blunt and revealing.

I thought and still do think the best thing that can be done for the young man is to make him an Indian trader, but Governor Simpson won't agree. He tells me the Company have determined to take none of these Young Men into their service.[22]

Somehow, however, Simpson's wishes had been overruled. John Junior had been accepted into the Company.

For a while Simpson did nothing to impede young McLoughlin's progress. But the relationship between Simpson and John McLoughlin Senior steadily deteriorated.

The fault was not entirely Simpson's. McLoughlin deliberately antagonized the Hudson's Bay Governor, perhaps because of the goading McLoughlin himself was receiving at the hands of the Hudson's Bay's Protestant chaplain Herbert Beaver.

It is interesting to note that during McLoughlin's first years as a gentleman of the Hudson's Bay Company he did not show himself to be a particularly religious man. In 1832 he was instrumental in obtaining the services of a New England teacher and lawyer, John Ball, to open the first school at Fort Vancouver, but he made no particular push to dictate to Ball whether religious instruction should be Protestant or Catholic, or indeed whether there should be religious instruction at all.

The arrival of Beaver changed that.

From the moment of his arrival at Fort Vancouver, Beaver deliberately provoked and antagonized McLoughlin over religious matters. McLoughlin retaliated, partly out of loyalty to his sister who was Mother Superior of a Roman Catholic convent in Quebec, partly out of sympathy for the underdog Roman Catholics who were a distinct minority among upper-level Hudson's Bay Company personnel, partly in direct reaction to Beaver whom he disliked intensely. The more Beaver goaded, the more determined McLoughlin became to push the cause of Roman Catholicism.

Inevitably, Simpson heard of it.

If Beaver was anti-Catholic, Simpson was doubly so. This fact was well known to everyone with whom Simpson came in contact. Now the knowledge that one of his top employees, the Chief Factor at Fort Vancouver, was publicly endorsing the cause of Catholicism, infuriated him.

The two men had already clashed over other issues. It was not surprising, for both were raw mannered, abrasive and dictatorial. The first clash occurred over the Company's decision to close Fort McLoughlin, a relatively new Hudson's Bay post named after the Chief Factor and established in 1833 on Milbanke Sound near Bella Bella. The next clash centred around the decision to relocate Fort Vancouver at a new site north of the 49th parallel. Now the issue was the American missionaries who were travelling up and down the Pacific coast.

For some time now, Simpson had been fearful of the influence of these American missionaries, and McLoughlin knew it. Simpson referred to them as "crafty and designing . . . likely to become very dangerous neighbors."[23] He saw them as possible United States agents with territorial designs on the Columbia territory. Accordingly, he issued orders that they should not be allowed into the Company trading posts in either Vancouver or Victoria.

Ordinarily, McLoughlin would have complied with those orders for he had no particular love for the American missionaries, but at that particular moment he was looking for a way to strike back at Governor Simpson.

A short time before, Herbert Beaver had announced that all the Fort children, Protestant and Catholic alike, must attend his Protestant church services. His purpose was obvious — before many weeks had passed he would be listing them as converts to the Protestant faith. To prevent this, McLoughlin retaliated by holding Roman Catholic masses at the same time as the Protestant services, conducting the masses himself.

If Simpson saw the American missionaries as possible United States agents with territorial designs on the Columbia territory, he saw every Roman Catholic as secretly working in the interests of France. He insisted that McLoughlin's services be stopped.

McLoughlin ignored him. Then to push home the message that he had no intention of giving in to Simpson, he contravened Simpson's orders concerning the American missionaries. He not only welcomed them to Fort Vancouver, but extended them unlimited credit at the Company store.

Against that background it is no wonder that Simpson had little sympathy for the problems John McLoughlin Junior was facing.

By this time young McLoughlin had been posted to Fort Stikine. Not only was Stikine one of the most remote and isolated of Hudson's Bay Company posts, it also had a reputation for being trouble-filled and hard to manage.

In the months after his arrival at Fort Stikine McLoughlin Junior wrote several times to his Company superiors voicing his uneasiness at being all alone in the northern post where "the Indians are very troublesome." He begged to be sent an assistant. He was ignored. So was a letter he sent to his friend Roderick Finlayson, Company Factor at Fort Simpson. "I am still among the living at this troublesome post," McLoughlin wrote, "though report says that I am soon going to be dispatched to the sandy hills." A subsequent letter from young McLoughlin stated, "If it was some other gentleman they would not be left so destitute as I have been. . . . I do not know what to do in the evening when I cannot sleep."[24]

Simpson paid no attention to any of this. Unfortunately, neither did anyone else.

On the evening of April 20th, 1842, John McLoughlin Junior was murdered.

The murder might have been avoided had Simpson or any other Company official paid attention to McLoughlin's letters. Certainly the guilty persons should have been punished and young John McLoughlin's name and reputation cleared. But because of Simpson's own intense prejudice against the offspring of mixed marriages and against Roman Catholics, when he arrived at Fort Stikine and was told by the men on the post that young McLoughlin had been drunk and had died as the result of a drunken fight, he made no attempt to investigate or to determine the truth of what had happened.

Simpson even refused to listen to valid testimony. Pierre Kanaquassé, one of the men involved, maintained under oath that during the entire term of John McLoughlin's service at Fort Stikine he had never been seen to be drunk. Kanaquassé went on to state that the enmity between the young Factor and his men arose as a direct result of his refusal to allow them to bring Indian women into the Fort or to leave it themselves for overnight visits. He insisted that any punishments McLoughlin had enacted had been fully justified, for the men had repeatedly "scaled the picquets" taking with them blankets and food stolen from the Company store as gifts for their Indian girl friends.[25]

Instead of recognizing the merit in what young McLoughlin had been attempting to accomplish, Simpson ignored Kanaquassé's testimony. He even ignored Kanaquassé's added statement that McLoughlin's murder had been premeditated. According to Kanaquassé as early as the fall of 1841 a paper had been drawn up and signed by all the men at Fort Stikine "agreeing to murder Mr. McLoughlin."[26]

It had been chance that had brought Governor Simpson on a routine visit to the Company post at Fort Stikine on the morning of April 20th, 1842. Word had not yet even been dispatched back to Company headquarters that Company trader John McLoughlin Junior had been murdered. Simpson arrived just hours after the incident had happened. He had a perfect opportunity to consider the evidence, question the fort personnel and determine exactly what had taken place. Instead he asked no questions but accepted the story of a dishevelled group of junior clerks that McLoughlin's death was the result of a drunken brawl which he himself had started.

The evidence disproving this was overwhelming. A full investigation should have been conducted and John McLoughlin's name cleared, but despite the pleas and the lobbying of John McLoughlin Senior, Simpson refused to discuss the case.

In this the Hudson's Bay Company concurred. Historian W. Kaye Lamb suggests this is not surprising. "Simpson was as nearly indispensable [to the Company] as an individual could be. To repudiate his views . . . publicly, was out of the question. . . . The Governor and Committee had no alternative but to stand behind him."[27]

It was a tragic incident, and reveals the extent to which religious intolerance in this far-west wilderness was capable of influencing decisions and warping judgement—capable of doing so even before the Men of God began arriving in any numbers and started vying with each other for converts. In 1842 when John McLoughlin was murdered, Father Demers and Father Blanchet were just beginning their residence in Victoria. Staines and Cridge had not yet arrived on the scene. The Columbia Mission had not yet been thought of. Admittedly, Beaver succeeded in fanning the fires of racial intolerance and bigotry during his two years at Fort Vancouver, but one man cannot be held responsible. Incidents such as the murder of John McLoughlin and the subsequent miscarriage of justice occurred because the potential for both racial and religious intolerance was woven into the very fabric and structure of fur-trade life.

†

Originally there had been two major fur-trading companies in the Canadian West—the Hudson's Bay Company and the North West Company. In 1821 they merged. The more affluent Hudson's Bay Company retained most of the power in decision-making and most of the top administrative posts, but the social structure of the newly expanded organization continued to be that established by the Nor'Westers.

The triple-level structure started with the trappers on the bottom. These men were drawn from all different First Nations tribes and followed many different faiths, but this was not a problem, for each man worked alone. He seldom came into contact with any of the other trappers and only rarely came into contact with any of the top-level officials. The only time he met any of them was when he came to deliver his furs, and that was a quick, stylized ritual with no opportunity for real communication. In no way, either as individuals or as members of a group, did these First Nations trappers have any opportunity to influence decisions or affect the structure of the fur trade.

The middle level of voyageurs were not isolated individuals like the trappers on the lower level. They were a tightly knit homogenous group, almost without exception young *Canadiens*. They were French-speaking and they were Roman Catholic. Because they were a closely knit group they had the potential to influence decision-making and to affect fur-trade structure if they had wanted to. The fact that they didn't do so was the result of the unique social class system that existed within the voyageur group itself, which provided stability, order and authority.

It consisted of five levels. At the bottom were those with least authority, the middle paddlers of the big canoes — *les mileux*. Next came *les avants*, or the front men. The third group were *les gouvernails* who stood at the back and directed passage. Fourth were *les guides*, and finally the top group who exerted the most authority and influence, the envied and respected *hivernants*, *les hommes du nord* who spent the winter beyond the fort, and who ate pemmican on the spring journeys instead of pork like the men of the other four classes.[28]

A novice voyageur started out as *un milieu*. His ambition was by hard work to climb to the rank of *hivernant*. He had neither the inclination nor the time to think about challenging the authority of the top level of the fur-trade hierarchy, the Company Traders.

It was at the Trader level that the potential for trouble within the fur-trade hierarchy existed, for this top level of Company traders, officers and fort personnel was not a homogenous group. Although the majority of these men were English-speaking Protestants, a significant minority were Roman Catholics. Here lay the threat to the solidarity of the fur-trade structure, for disagreements and grievances were inevitable.

During the first years after the merger the disagreements were carefully played down. The situation changed, however, with the introduction of the first Hudson's Bay chaplains. First Beaver, then Staines, made religion a matter for open debate and confrontation.

Suddenly the three distinct and separate compartments within fur-trade society were no longer distinct and separate. The thick walls that had kept them apart began disintegrating. Ties of Protestant to Protestant or Catholic to Catholic began to supersede distinctions of trapper, voyageur, or Company official. Before anyone quite realized what was happening holes had been driven into the floors and ceilings that heretofore had separated the three levels. No longer was the authority of the top level absolute. No longer were the two lower levels of the hierarchy isolated and silent.

Trouble might have been postponed at least for a while had Beaver and Staines behaved as the Company had envisaged, and provided the services of the Protestant Church to those who asked but left the others alone. But both men were determined to convert everyone to their faith.

"The Missionary must be cool and temperate . . . of a mild conciliatory disposition," Simpson had warned several years earlier. He ". . . should place himself under the protection of the . . . Chief Factor, and look up to that gentleman for support and assistance in everything."[29]

If he had hoped that his advice would be heeded, Simpson should have hired someone other than Herbert Beaver as his first far-west chaplain, or sent him to work under someone other than McLoughlin.

The conflict between Beaver and McLoughlin began within a day of the new Hudson's Bay chaplain's arrival. It began over the school.

There had been a small school at Fort Vancouver since 1832 run by John Ball, a New England teacher who had come west to Oregon looking for work and had welcomed McLoughlin's invitation to come to Fort Vancouver and start a school there. Upon Beaver's arrival, however, McLoughlin compliantly turned control of the school over to him, but not without reservation. Prompted by the urgings of his sister, he stipulated that any religious training that had already been started with any of the fort children was not to be interfered with. He then gave Beaver a school register in which more than ninety per cent of the names were accompanied by the initial C to indicate that the children were already established Catholics.

Beaver was incensed. He considered the area of Fort Vancouver to be his parish, and according to the rules of the Church of England, a parish rector had full jurisdiction over the parish school. Moreover, a clergyman of the Church of England took orders from no one but his bishop or his squire. McLoughlin was neither. Accordingly, Beaver felt no compulsion to obey, particularly when an investigation revealed that no more than three or four of those students listed by McLoughlin as Catholics, could be proven to be so.

He reminded McLoughlin that he had been brought to Fort Vancouver to serve as chaplain and schoolteacher, and that he therefore had full jurisdiction over the pupils. He went on to add that irrespective of what the school register might say, he expected all of them to attend his daily Protestant church services.

That was when McLoughlin instituted Roman Catholic mass at the same time as Beaver's services, either conducting mass himself or having David Dompier do so, a devout Roman Catholic layman.

Beaver took the power struggle a step farther. Now he attacked McLoughlin on the personal level, through his First Nations wife. Claiming the authority of an ordained clergyman, he denounced all unchurched fur-trade unions. Marriage *à la façon du pays* was not true marriage, he insisted, for marriage was a sacrament of the church.

He shaped his attack so that it was aimed at all unchurched fur-trade unions, but his main purpose was to criticize two of them—Governor James Douglas's and Chief Factor John McLoughlin's.

The inherent problem of introducing a chaplain into a society that condoned out-of-wedlock unions was something Simpson had foreseen. Despite his bias against the First Nations people and against the offspring of mixed marriages, and despite his clearly expressed opinion that such offspring should never be employed by the Company, he was astute enough to recognize the value in the "marriages" themselves. How else could the Company hope to keep the men from leaving these remote posts? Accordingly he added to his list of requirements for potential Company chaplains the injunction that chaplains should view with tolerance and leniency the possible moral impropriety of such "marriages."

"Nearly all the Gentlemen and Servants have families, although Marriage ceremonies are unknown," Simpson stated. "But it would be all in vain to attempt breaking through this uncivilized custom."[30]

Beaver, however, paid no attention. He refused to recognize the danger that his actions would pose to the stability of the fur trade itself, and began a concerted attack on all unchurched fur-trade unions. First he proposed that all wives of such unions should have their rations stopped, and that they should be denied all free medical attention. Then he began an insidious program of harassment and badgering. The result was that within six months a significant number of fort personnel agreed to legalize their common-law unions with a proper church ceremony. Beaver even convinced James Douglas to remarry his half-breed wife, Amelia Connolly, in a proper Church of England ceremony. And when Chief Factor McLoughlin's pretty, half-breed daughter, Maria Eloise, married trader William Glen Rae, Beaver was allowed to perform the ceremony.

But as far as McLoughlin's own marriage was concerned, the Chief Factor remained adamant. Had there been an ordained Roman Catholic priest in the region McLoughlin would no doubt have agreed willingly to a church ceremony, but the arrival of the first Roman Catholic missionaries in the Fort Vancouver area was still several years away. It was Beaver or nothing, and there was no way the Hudson's Bay Chief Factor would allow Beaver the psychological advantage that would inevitably ensue if he submitted to an Anglican service. Also, he considered his marriage *à la façon du pays* to be already legally binding. In this he was justified. A few years later the Supreme Court of Quebec ruled in favour of that very thing. There was still another reason why McLoughlin felt a church ceremony was unnecessary. He had already had a follow-up civil marriage ceremony performed by James Douglas in his office as Chief Justice. In McLoughlin's opinion, his marriage had received all the formalization it required.

It was not just over religious matters that Beaver showed himself to be hot tempered and arrogant. From the moment he had arrived in Fort Vancouver he had complained. First it was because no provision had been made for a proper reception for himself and his wife. Then it was that their quarters were inadequate, with noisy neighbours, and with the public route to the Company storage area accessible only through their living quarters. Finally he objected to the "incompetent servant" assigned to them, to the "meagreness of their wine allowance," and to the "stubbornness of the cook" who refused to cook salmon in the way in which his wife was accustomed to eating it.[31]

Had Simpson looked carefully into the background of Herbert Beaver before hiring him as the first far-west Company chaplain he might have guessed that there would be trouble. An item in the marriage register at Castries, a parish in the British West Indies where Beaver had been both rector and Army chaplain immediately before coming to Canada, gives some insight into the possessiveness of Beaver's personality. It was written by the man sent to replace Beaver as rector.

"I hereby certify that the above is a true correct copy of a register made by me on the day of the marriage, I being prevented from entering it into the proper book by Mr. Beaver, the late minister, keeping violent possession of the same and refusing to give it to me."[32]

Simpson obviously had not been aware of the item, or if he was, disregarded it.

Beaver, meantime, found new things to complain about. Now it was that the church building he had been promised before he had left England had never materialized, with the result that he was forced to hold services in the fort mess hall. Then he received a request from some French-speaking residents of the fort for Church of England services in the French language. Beaver was delighted, but before he could act on the request, found himself in open confrontation with McLoughlin, who was determined to prevent him from doing so.

The final blow for Beaver came when McLoughlin announced he had decided to replace him as teacher in the fort school. The insult might not have been as severe if Simpson had chosen a Roman Catholic as the new schoolteacher, but McLoughlin instead put control of the fort school into the hands of the wives of two visiting Congregationalist ministers, Mrs. Narcissa Whitman (killed nine years later in the "Whitman Massacre") and Mrs. Henry Spalding.[33]

Beaver wrote a scorching letter to the Company officials in London defending his position and accusing McLoughlin of injustice and wrong-doing. To clinch his case he attacked McLoughlin's character, included a comment describing McLoughlin's wife as ". . . a female of notoriously loose character . . . the kept mistress of the highest personage in your service at this station."

It was several months before the contents of this letter became known to McLoughlin. By this time relations between the two men had deteriorated to the point where they no longer spoke to each other. If communication on some issue was absolutely necessary they sent messages through Beaver's wife, Jane, or through Company official James Douglas. But silence was forgotten on the morning that McLoughlin learned of the contents of Beaver's letter.

The meeting of the two men on the dirt of the fort compound was described in detail by Beaver some time later as part of the plea he presented in Court in an attempt to collect his back salary.

> I was walking across the fort yard to talk to my wife who was standing at the door of our house, when this monster in human form . . . advanced upon us, apparently in a violent passion, and upon my making way for him to pass he came up behind me, kicked me several times, and struck me repeatedly with his fists in the back of the neck.
>
> Unable to cope with him from the immense disparity of our relative size and strength, I could not prevent him from wrenching out of my hands a stout stick with which I was walking, and with which he next inflicted several severe blows on my shoulders. He then seized me from behind around my waist and attempted to dash me to the ground, exclaiming, "You scoundrel! I will have your life!"
>
> In the meantime the stick had fallen to the ground; my wife on the impulse of the moment picked it up; he took it, to use the epithet of an eye-witness, "very viciously" out of her hands and again struck me with it severely.
>
> We were then separated by the intervention of other persons.[34]

A few days after this incident McLoughlin sailed for England. Beaver wanted to follow. He knew McLoughlin would be presenting his side of the dispute to the Governor and Committee in London and wanted to present his own case. In his own words he wanted to inform the Committee about the conditions he had faced ever since his arrival in Fort Vancouver, ". . . how fruitless was my mission from want of support . . . how I was in a stronghold of Popery, defended and sustained by John M'Loughlin [sic] . . . how my wife and I were subject to much personal insult and domestic annoyance."[35] But he could not secure passage on any vessel. It was a full six months before he could find anyone who would take him, by which time the Committee had listened to McLoughlin's argument and agreed on their decision. Beaver was given no opportunity to plead his case. He was simply informed by the Governor and Committee that the Company "had no further occasion" for his services.

"I had by no means meant to vacate my appointment by leaving Vancouver," he wrote later in his own defence, "but had done so with the sole intention, if not redress for the past, security at least for the future. But all indemnity was refused; even the full discharge of my hardly-earned salary."[36]

Beaver had been resident in Fort Vancouver as the Hudson's Bay's first far-west chaplain for only two years, but the repercussions resulting from that two-year residence are considerable.

✝

It required ten years of debate before the Hudson's Bay Company decided to bring a second chaplain to this far-west wilderness. The man they finally selected was Robert John Staines, a schoolteacher, not a clergyman.

Staines was hired solely to fill the position of schoolteacher at Fort Vancouver. It was not until the Company was interviewing him and discovered that he considered "religious instruction in accordance with the doctrines of the Church of England as an indispensable part of a sound education,"[37] that it occurred to them that he might combine the office of schoolteacher with that of fort chaplain. It seemed an excellent plan for both sides. Staines could supplement his teaching salary with an additional one hundred pounds per annum, and the Company would have the services of a chaplain at very little cost. Accordingly, with no clerical training, Staines was admitted to Holy Orders.

On September 12, 1848, Staines, his wife and ten-year-old nephew, Horace Tahourdin, left London for Fort Vancouver. Seven months later after an interminable sea voyage during which Staines was exceedingly sick, they found they had been posted not to the settled and relatively comfortable Fort Vancouver as they had expected, but to the Hudson's Bay post of Fort Victoria instead.

Roderick Finlayson, then Factor in charge of Fort Victoria, describes their arrival.

> There were no streets . . . Everyone had to wear sea boots to wade through the mud and mire. We had to lay planks through the mud in order to get them [Staines and his wife] safely to the fort.
> They looked around wonderingly at the bare walls of the buildings, and expressed deep surprise, stating that the Co. [*sic*] in England had told them this and that, and had promised such and such.[38]

The disappointment Staines and his wife felt at sight of their new home was soon equalled by that felt by fort personnel over their new chaplain. Unquestionably, Staines's academic qualifications were above reproach. Testimonials exist applauding his proficiency as a classical scholar, as a mathematics lecturer and as a critic of English literature. He is cited as having an "aptitude for communication that is so necessary for the instruction of youth."[39] His wife was equally well qualified. In addition to proficiency in music, she was fluent in French, German and Italian, as well as English. However, in other areas both Staines and his wife were found to be singularly unsuited for missionary service.

As Beaver had clashed almost immediately with Chief Factor McLoughlin, so Staines now clashed with James Douglas. First it was about the failure of the Company to provide a separate home for himself and his wife. Then he picked up the issue raised earlier by Beaver about the need for a separate church building. He had brought with him from England a commission authorizing him to consecrate a church and a cemetery, and he took this as proof that a church was to be built. However, Hudson's Bay Governor James Douglas refused even to discuss it. "It is no part of my plan that the Company should be put to the charge of providing churches and schoolhouses," he informed Staines in a letter dated August 27, 1850. "I recommend leaving such matters to the inhabitants themselves."[40]

Next, Staines's competency as a teacher came under attack, not for his scholastic qualifications but because of his temperament. He was accused by several parents of being "unduly severe in administering corporal punishment." The accusations were justified for Staines was strict to the point of brutality, and so was his wife. James Robert Anderson, son of Chief Factor A. C. Anderson and one of Staines's early pupils describes with horror his memories of life at the school. From early morning till late evening the days were filled with interminable prayer sessions, long morning church services, even longer afternoon church services, and the time in between was spent memorizing the Collects. Any boys who fell asleep despite the hard benches were severely beaten.[41]

Eventually the protests of pupils and parents, strengthened by a threat to withhold all further financial support for the school unless Staines should be replaced, prodded the Hudson's Bay Company into action, but not before Staines, like his predecessor Beaver, initiated the first of a series of moves which affected significantly on social, political, legal and moral issues.

His first move was a campaign to deliberately discredit both the territorial government and the Hudson's Bay Company. He set this in motion by collecting names on a petition and sending it to Governor Blanshard defaming James Douglas. He accompanied this petition with a letter strongly urging the Governor to strip Douglas of authority, and to delegate no further authority to him.

Next he sent an "anonymous" letter to the Colonial Office in London condemning the oppressive conditions that existed on Vancouver Island and holding the Hudson's Bay Company and James Douglas directly responsible for them. Not content with that, when James Douglas's brother-in-law, David Cameron, was made Chief Justice of British Columbia, Staines began circulating accusations that the colony was being run by a "Family Compact."

Staines's personal relations with the Company were already strained. He was deeply in debt, consistently overcharging at the Company store, and still owed the money he had borrowed to finance his trip to Canada. He also owed in full for the farm land he had "bought" on Company credit on his arrival in Victoria. He had decided he wasn't going to repay that part of his debt at all. He based his argument on the fact that the land agreement by which the Hudson's Bay Company held all the land on Vancouver Island was about to expire. It was expected that when this happened the government would reclaim all the territory, in which case, Staines insisted, there was no need for him to repay any money to the Hudson's Bay Company.

Staines was also embroiled in a court case over some pigs which he was accused of having stolen. It subsequently turned out that the pigs were his own and he was cleared of the accusation, but not before his behaviour in court had seriously damaged his reputation both as a schoolteacher and as a cleric.

In August 1853 the Hudson's Bay Company officially notified Staines that his services as schoolmaster were no longer needed, but they did not relieve him of his office as chaplain. "We should consider it derogatory to the reputation of the Company to visit Mr. Staines with dismissal from the office of chaplain," Deputy Governor John Shepherd wrote privately to James Douglas.[42]

It was small comfort to Staines. More determined than ever to discredit both James Douglas and the Hudson's Bay Company, Staines volunteered to go to London as spokesman for a small group of local residents who wanted to protest the appointment of Cameron as Chief Justice. Staines offered to represent them, intending at the same time to present his larger case against the Company and its Governor. But his plan miscarried. Within days of leaving Victoria the vessel he was sailing on foundered and sank in heavy seas. Everyone on board, including Staines, was drowned.

Like Beaver, Staines, too, had remained in the far west for only a short time but his impact on the newly emerging region was significant. Not only did he succeed in igniting local opinion against James Douglas and David Cameron, he also succeeded in spreading misgivings in Britain about the successful administration of the colony.

†

Despite the problems caused by Beaver and Staines, the Hudson's Bay Company optimistically began initiating plans to bring in yet another chaplain. They settled on the Reverend Edward Cridge. Two years after the departure of Staines, Cridge took over as the Hudson's Bay's third far-west chaplain.

As it turned out he was also their last — not because the Hudson's Bay Company had learned to be wary of catalyst chaplains, but because by now it was apparent even to the Hudson's Bay Company that the provision of religious leadership was no longer their responsibility. The established churches were ready and willing to take over. By the time Cridge arrived, Roman Catholic Fathers Demers and Blanchet had already been established in the Victoria area for more than a decade. Three years after Cridge's appointment, Anglican cleric Burton Crickmer arrived, followed the next year by Congregationalist William F. Clarke. Then in 1859, the Columbia Mission was established, its mandate to bring Christianity to the whole territory west of the Canadian Rockies.

Caveat emptor. If Beaver and Staines had caused waves, now the far-west was about to be shaken up in earnest.

Chapter 3

THE COLUMBIA MISSION

WITH SO MANY missionaries from various denominations arriving in this far-west wilderness, it might have been expected that they would vie with each other to influence and direct the path that emerging political, judicial and social patterns were to take. Particularly, it might have been expected that the two churches with the largest number of missionaries—the Roman Catholic and the Anglican—would compete to see which could exert the strongest influence as catalysts and watchdogs.

This did not happen. The Anglican clerics accepted the challenge and fulfilled this role, as, subsequently, did the Methodists and Congregationalists, but the Roman Catholic missionaries did not. Instead they tended to restrict themselves to parochial duties, concentrating on addressing the spiritual needs of their people, and avoided becoming involved in debates and decision-making concerning political, judicial and economic issues.

One reason for this might be rooted in nineteenth-century Roman Catholic missionary methodology. At that time it was expected that all the missionaries of the Roman Catholic Church would act in accordance with the prescribed pattern for missionary activity set down by their church. The rules were common for Roman Catholic missionaries anywhere in the world, and made no allowances for differing conditions or unusual problems.[43] Innovation, or individual interpretation on the part of a missionary was discouraged. So was the expression of a missionary's personal opinion. Missionaries were not encouraged to develop their own particular techniques for achieving any particular end, nor were they encouraged to deviate from the prescribed pattern for missionary activity, even though local conditions or individual problems might make such deviation seem advisable. In the light of this, it is perhaps not surprising that most of the Roman Catholic missionaries in Canada's far west during the crucial years prior to B.C.'s entering Confederation refrained from getting involved in general issues and concerned themselves instead with the spiritual needs of their parishioners, a responsibility for which they had received clearly set out instructions and codes of conduct.

Another factor which may have played a part was that during much of the critical period between 1858 and 1871 when those issues were being decided that would eventually determine the shape of the future province of British Columbia, Bishop Demers was not free to become involved even if he had wanted to. He was preoccupied with a power struggle of his own.

It centred around Roman Catholic Oblate Father Louis D'herbomez. The Roman Catholic missionary had come west to work in Oregon as leader and spokesman for a group of Oblate Fathers. The area was already under the supervision of Oregon's Roman Catholic bishops, but D'herbomez refused to work under them. He insisted that the Oblates should be put in charge of their own area and that within that area they should have complete autonomy. Oregon's bishops refused. Accordingly, D'herbomez moved his Oblates into Canada's far west.

At first Victoria's Roman Catholic Bishop Modeste Demers welcomed them, for at that time he had no resident diocesan priests of his own. Had he and the newly arrived group of Oblates been able to work together they might have exerted their influence on developing social and political policy despite the restrictions of nineteenth-century Roman Catholic missionary methodology. But they couldn't work together. D'herbomez's major concern was still autonomy for his Oblates. Having avoided the supervisory control of the Oregon bishops, he had no wish to fall under the supervision of a Canadian one. Rather than working with Demers, he asked the Victoria bishop to relinquish his authority over the area of New Caledonia and to put this region under the control of the Oblates, using as his argument the urgent need for more mainland Roman Catholic missions.

Demers, of course, refused. Up until now the entire far-west region had been included in his Roman Catholic diocese and he wanted it to stay that way.

D'herbomez, however, was not easily discouraged. He referred the dispute to church authorities in Rome. In 1864 it was finally settled. Despite Demers's protests, church authorities sided with D'herbomez.

They took the region of New Caledonia away from Demers and gave it to the Oblates as the Vicariate of British Columbia[44] with D'herbomez as the newly consecrated "Bishop of the Melitopolis."

The lengthy struggle before the issue was settled, the ensuing dissatisfaction, and the subsequent re-organization occurred just when contentious political, social and legal issues were starting to surface. Even if Demers or D'herbomez or any of the missionaries under their authority had wanted to involve themselves in confrontation with political, social and judicial leaders, they would not have been free to do so.

One other factor may have contributed to the reluctance of the Roman Catholic missionaries to join the Anglicans, Methodists and Congregationalists in political debate and confrontation. That is their difference in background and upbringing. During these early years when policies were being decided that would affect the eventual shape of British Columbia, the Protestant missionaries in Canada's far west were men from upper-class homes with Oxford or Cambridge educations. They were eloquent speakers, accustomed to moving in the same circles as politicians, cabinet ministers and judges, and quite prepared to debate with any of them about contentious issues.

Most of the Roman Catholic missionaries, on the other hand, were not from upper-class homes. They were men of modest education from middle-class homes in Quebec or rural France. They were not at home with cabinet ministers or judges, and many of them spoke English as a second language. It is not surprising that they should have hesitated to engage men like James Douglas and Matthew Baillie Begbie in verbal debate.

But while the Roman Catholic missionaries may have refrained from involving themselves in contentious political and judicial issues, the Protestant missionaries did not.

Wesleyan Thomas Crosby played watchdog and catalyst from the moment he arrived in the Canadian west, eventually becoming such a strong voice of protest against the fledgeling government's first moves in the land title conflict, that he was legally banned from attending any more hearings. Methodist Arthur Browning challenged prestigious Judge Matthew Begbie Baillie head on. Congregationalist missionary William F. Clarke tackled Governor James Douglas within days of his arrival in Victoria over the issue of government control of the church. With the assistance of *Daily Courier* editor William Alexander Smith, later to take the name Amor De Cosmos, Clarke succeeded in forcing the formidable colonial Governor to back down. Anglican Bishop George Hills proved to be one of the most outspoken catalysts and watchdogs of all.

Hills arrived in Victoria on January 6th, 1860, after a sea voyage of three months. Prior to his arrival the number of missionaries in the Victoria area included Congregationalist William F. Clarke, Anglican Burton Crickmer, Hudson's Bay chaplain Edward Cridge, Roman Catholic Bishop Modeste Demers, Father D'herbomez, Father Rondeault, Father Donkele, and four Sisters of St. Anne. With Hills's arrival the number almost doubled, for he did not come alone. The Columbia Mission sent six other Anglican clerics with him.

The impact of this group was considerable, for they were not a collection of independently functioning missionaries. They were a unified group under strong leadership. They also had the advantage of knowing they had the financial and psychological backing of the whole Church of England. Should the actions of a Hudson's Bay factor need to be criticized, should a brake need to be put on the decision of some government official, judge or land commissioner, the missionaries of the Columbia Mission felt no hesitation in providing that criticism or applying that brake. Rather than being expected to conform to prescribed patterns of behaviour as were the Roman Catholic missionaries, the Anglicans were expected to lead, to make decisions, to criticize and to set standards.

They did. Particularly George Hills.

Hills was a man of intense religious conviction; he was also self-assured and opinionated. Perhaps this is not surprising, for he had been singled out to undertake the job of converting this huge area to Anglicanism by the most respected and prestigious woman in Victorian England next to the Queen herself—Angela Burdett-Coutts. Such public endorsement was tantamount to a knighthood, for Miss Burdett-Coutts (later to be Baroness) had inherited a huge fortune from her banker grandfather and moved in the highest circles. She was a friend of Gladstone and Disraeli, and was linked romantically with the ageing Duke of Wellington. She attended scientific lectures in the company of Sir Michael Faraday and was a close personal friend of Dickens. In fact, she admitted to being the "lady unknown" whom Dickens often credited with particularly generous donations to his charities.[45] As a result, when on her recommendation the Columbia Mission sent Hills out to do their work on the Canadian frontier they did so with unrealistically high expectations.

This in itself was to cause problems, for George Hills was a strange mixture—autocratic, snobbish and dictatorial on the one hand, sensitive and insecure on the other. The strength of his convictions made it difficult for him to see more than one side to an issue. The strict self-imposed rules which governed his own conduct made it impossible for him to condone anyone else's moral weakness. The demands he made on himself and the high goals he set caused him to expect the same commitment from everyone around him. His strengths seemed to form a barrier between himself and his clergy, and he was a lonely man. "I do not think my clergy look up to their Bishop," he writes in the faithfully kept journal that at times seemed to be more of a confessional than an historical record. "I am not a true head over them."[46]

Some of the problems Hills had with his clergy can be linked to the publicity that attended his selection as first Anglican bishop of this remote area. That publicity guaranteed that everything Hills did would be watched and commented upon by influential people in England. Determined not to incur any criticism, Hills sometimes sacrificed personal relationships in favour of being seen publicly to uphold the rules.

One of the clergy who had been awaiting Hills's arrival in January 1860 was Hudson's Bay chaplain Edward Cridge. Cridge had come to Victoria five years earlier after the departure of Staines, and with the exception of Burton Crickmer who arrived late in 1858, had been the only Church of England cleric in the entire far-west region. It was probably with some misgivings that Cridge welcomed the new bishop, for Cridge was outspoken and self-confident, and had run his church for five years without any episcopal supervision. However, he knew the rules of the Anglican Church, and when a controversial issue arose shortly after Hills arrived in Victoria, Cridge referred the matter to the bishop.

It concerned a request Cridge had received from one of his parishioners to conduct a wedding service at a time other than that permitted by the canons of the Anglican Church. According to the canons in existence at that time marriages could only be conducted between 8 and 12 a.m. unless special permission was granted by the Archbishop of Canterbury. Any clergyman breaking this rule was in danger of suspension from his duties for a period of three years.[47] However, the precedent had been established that in special cases any bishop, not just the Archbishop of Canterbury, could give permission for this rule to be waived. Cridge wanted Hills to do this, for a parishioner was being sent away unexpectedly and wished to be married that afternoon.

Hills hedged. Constrained, no doubt, by fear of censure from the church at home, he sent a lengthy letter of explanation to Cridge but still gave no firm directive. Half the points in his letter favoured relaxing the canon, the other half favoured maintaining it. In his journal he admitted, "I said I had no power to grant any indulgence from the rule of the Canon [*sic*], but that if the case was one of emergency, I should take no notice if on his own he [Cridge] chose to perform the ceremony."

Indecisiveness characterized Hills's whole relationship with Edward Cridge, and twelve years later culminated in a final conflict between them that saw Cridge break completely from the Anglican Church and start a new church of his own. The motivating incident was Hills's changing his mind about a concert in Cridge's church to raise money. Having originally given approval for the concert, Hills then cancelled it, completely ignoring the fact that the reason the concert had been planned was to try to reduce some of the debt under which the church laboured and for which Hills himself was largely responsible.

Again the enigmatic, multi-sided personality of Hills is evident, for though he fought Cridge single-mindedly, even through an ecclesiastical court case that was criticized afterward with some justification for being suspect, once he had won and Cridge had left the Anglican Church, Hills never stopped berating himself for his part in events. His journal entries during the years that followed are filled with self-doubt and self-recrimination.

Second thoughts and mind-changing characterized many of Hills's relationships. A basic inbred conservatism that had always characterized him and made him hesitant to commit himself on controversial issues was magnified after his appointment as Bishop of Columbia by the knowledge that everything he did was being watched and criticized.

This was evident early in 1861 when the church was given the chance to buy a large section of downtown Victoria property. A large profit could have been made, which the fledgeling church needed, but the property included a theatre. Fearful that criticism might be directed at him for linking the church's name with such a property, Hills turned down the opportunity, despite the urging of all his advisors.[48]

The same fear of public censure revealed itself when three prominent Victoria residents, all members of Hills's church, approached him on behalf of an inexperienced young colonial treasurer named Gordon. There had been a minor misuse of funds, and Messrs. Trutch, Crease and Green approached Hills asking him to buy young Gordon's farm so he could replace the money before his career was ruined. The understanding was that as soon as Gordon could manage it, he would buy the farm back again.

Hills wanted to agree, for Gordon had a wife and seven children to support, but his fear of public censure should the matter ever become public made him hesitate. He still had not made up his mind what he should do when news of the defalcation became public and Gordon was arrested.

On the other hand, Hills could, on occasion, be both decisive and sympathetic. In 1861, less than a year after refusing to give Cridge any firm directive about performing marriages after 12 noon, Hills gave official permission for the Reverend R. J. Dundas to perform an evening ceremony. The groom was seriously ill. Noting in his journal that the bride was a mature woman and that the marriage might save the man's life, Hills gave official permission for the marriage to be performed immediately in the groom's bedchamber.

He also, on occasion, revealed traces of a sense of humour. During his second year as Bishop of Columbia he included in his journal an account of a visit paid to him by a smart young lady. At this time Hills was still a bachelor. According to his hand-written account the young lady first apologized for coming, asked Hills to hold in confidence what she was about to say, then burst out,

> The fact is that I have had a great many offers. There are several gentlemen wishing to marry me, but I did not like to give a positive answer to any of them until I had found out your mind. If you would like to have me, I would much prefer you to any of them.

The journal entry ends with Hills's comment, "You may consider the Bishop's amused embarrassment."[49]

Such instances of being able to laugh at himself were rare, however. For the most part Hills had a dread of public censure and worried about what people thought of him. He criticized himself openly in his journal. The entry on the fifth anniversary of his consecration as a Bishop reads:

> The impression of my unfitness for my office has increased as the years have gone on. In these times the Bishop needs to be a learned man to drive away erroneous teaching. In this I am most deficient. . . . In conversation with Society I am sadly deficient for I fear to bring my office into contempt.

On his initial shipboard journey to British Columbia Hills had met a Yorkshireman with whom he had enjoyed many discussions. Some months later when they met in Victoria, the Yorkshireman accused Hills of having changed. "I was pleased with thee aboard the steamer and liked thy liberality, but now they say thee art a Puseyite." The Yorkshireman used the term to mean someone so prejudiced they could not even talk to anyone who disagreed with them.

Obviously the accusation hurt, for over a year later Hills was still thinking about it. An entry in his journal on that date notes that he had again discussed the matter with Christopher Knipe, one of his clergy, and had been assured that he was not a Puseyite.[50]

Unquestionably, Hills had some difficulty communicating with his clergy. Perhaps part of the problem stemmed from Hills's upper-class, nineteenth-century upbringing. Like many boys of his class he had been educated at elitist public schools where young men were encouraged to hide their feelings under an impassive exterior. Perhaps it was as a result of this early training that Hills found it difficult to express his feelings and was uncomfortable in the presence of other people's emotion. The result was that he went out of his way to avoid any expression of feelings.

In many cases the results were unfortunate. A young man named Harvey had volunteered for missionary service and came to the far west among one of the first groups of missionaries. Enthusiastic but inexperienced, Harvey was unprepared for the seemingly interminable sea voyage and the impossible living conditions aboard ship. By the time the ship docked in Victoria, he was being branded by his fellow travellers as a drunkard.

The news soon reached Hills, who was expecting the new arrivals. The Bishop gave Harvey no opportunity to explain. In fact he avoided any direct meeting with him at all. Making no allowance for the fact that Harvey, much younger than any of the other men, had been the butt of their jokes and odd-man-out in every discussion, or that he had been frightened and homesick, Hills announced unequivocally that the man had no place in missionary work, and would not even be allowed to attend church services during the time it would take to make arrangements to send him home again by means of another lengthy sea voyage.

It was a crushing punishment, for the following Sunday was Easter. According to the rubric of the Anglican Prayer Book every confirmed member of the Anglican Church was expected to make his communion at least three times each year, one of which times must be Easter. Failing to do so repudiated one of the rules of church membership. For Hills to demand this of a young man who was hoping to enter the ministry seems unnecessarily severe.

"I did it with sorrow," Hills admits in his journal entry for April 8th, 1860. "I felt, however, that it was of great importance that we should avoid scandal, and not allow anyone to enter our mission circle whose character was sullied." A further note the next day read, "I must keep the sacred ministry free from blemish."

At last when Eastertide was over Hills did go to speak in person with Harvey. That meeting, described in his journal dated April 28th, explains at least partially his action.

Poor Harvey . . . is much troubled by his prospects. His emotion is to me a great affliction, yet I am every day more and more convinced of the propriety of my course, and how fortunate was the discovery of intemperance before I admitted him to Holy Orders.

Another factor that complicated Hills's relationships with his clergy was the fact that he tended to intimidate the men working under him. Hills wrote repeatedly in his journal about how difficult life was for the clergy in the Canadian far west, and how disillusioned and disheartened many of them were becoming, but he seemed unable to get them to discuss these problems with him on a personal basis.

When Christopher Knipe volunteered for Columbia Mission work in 1861, for example, Hills was delighted. Knipe was exactly the kind of man he had been looking for—an upper-class Englishman with an excellent education and an attractive personality. In addition Knipe was financially independent, and had volunteered to come to Canada at his own expense. Hills put him to work first in the gold mine camps where he was confident Knipe's enthusiasm and education would earn a ready response from the miners, then moved him to Alberni. For the next three and a half years all Hills's comments concerning Knipe in his reports back to London and in his journal were positive and untroubled. He applauded Knipe for his hard work and his enthusiasm, and he praised him as an excellent preacher. There was no suggestion anywhere that anything might be wrong.

Then as Hills was returning to Canada from a trip back to England in 1865 his ship stopped to reprovision in San Francisco. The British Consul informed him that Mr. Knipe was now a resident of that city.

Hills was amazed, for the term of Knipe's missionary contract had still another year to run. He sent word to Knipe through the British Consul that he was in town and asked Knipe to come to see him.

But as the day advanced he [Knipe] did not come to see me. I heard he was at an Hotel called the American Exchange, so I called. He came down, then started back on seeing me. He looked the picture of misery. He had allowed the hair to grow on his face and did not know what to say.[51]

Hills later admits that he had heard casual mention of problems in the Alberni district where Knipe had been working, and that he was vaguely aware that the mission was in some danger of closing, but apparently he made no attempt to discuss the matter with Knipe, and Knipe must have been too ill-at-ease with his bishop to initiate the discussion himself.

In the same way it did not seem to occur to Hills that James Reynard, the Anglican missionary he sent to Barkerville at the height of the gold rush, might also need advice and encouragement, for the situation Reynard faced in the Canadian north was almost more than any man could endure. But when a complete breakdown, both physical and mental, finally forced Reynard to abandon his work, Hills's chief concern seemed to be to ensure that the missionary societies in England understood it was Reynard who was responsible for the huge debt incurred by building a church in the gold town of Barkerville and not the diocese of British Columbia.

Once again Hills's preoccupation with his own reputation in England and with any possible censure that might be directed at him from the influential people there seemed to take precedence over his concern for the welfare of his missionary clergy and the churches they were struggling to establish.

Sir George Simpson, 1857

Dr. John McLoughlin

The First
(Anglican)
Christ Church
Victoria, B.C.

Begun 1853;
Opened 1856 and
Destroyed by
fire 1869.

ARCHIVES DES CHÂTRECETS

Bishop D'Herbomez

A young George Hills

Holy Trinity, New Westminster 1860

Angela Burdett-Coutts

A typical road house of the era. Kanaka Bar Hotel built 1858.

Father James McGuckin

Rev. Christopher
Knipe

BCARS: 6177

Old Lytton
Jail
built 1860.
Used by
Judge Matthew
Begbie

ARCHIVES OF THE ANGLICAN DIOCESE OF CARIBOO

Rev. John Sheepshanks, *c.* 1860.

Rev. Ephriam Evans

BCCA: 1-58

Methodist Church and Parsonage next to the Church of England, St. Saviour's, Barkerville, 1898.

Methodist Parsonage or Manse. Used as bachelor's quarters by Dawson H. Elliott, the Barkerville school teacher and Rev. H. J. Pritchard, D.D., Barkerville, 1890s.

St. Saviour's, Barkerville.

Rev. James Reynard suffered greatly with his family at Barkerville
and was the original builder of St. Saviour's.

Bishop Edward Cridge of the Reformed Episcopal Church.

Bishop George Hills.

Front, Crosby Girls'
Home, Port Simpson.

BCCA 2-978

Group of children outside
Crosby Mission House.

BCCA 2-996

Port Simpson,
left: Girls' Home,
centre: Mission
House, *right*:
Boys' Home.

BCCA 979

Girls with teacher.

Miss Hart and
Miss Ross with girls, 1888.

Rev. Thomas and
Mrs. Emma Crosby in
retirement in Vancouver.

Bishop
Acton W. Sillitoe

ANGLICAN
PROVINCIAL
SYNOD OF B.C.

Andrew Onderdonk's residence at Yale, later All Hallows School.

Native pupils and teachers, All Hallows.

Pupils, teachers and staff, All Hallows, 1886.

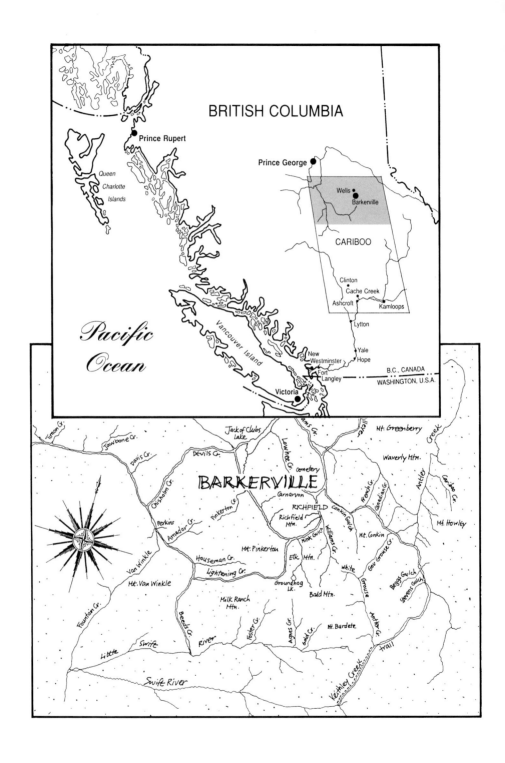

Chapter 4

MISSIONS TO THE MINERS

THE STORY of the Men of God in the gold fields is one of hardship, perseverance and endurance. It is also one of accomplishment.

In 1856, three years before the establishment of the Columbia Mission, gold was discovered on the Thompson River by a native as he was scooping up water for a drink.[52] Little attention was paid to the find.

Two years later gold was discovered on a sandbar in the Fraser River ten miles upstream from Hope, and this time a great deal of attention was paid to it. Before the end of that year every sandbar in the Fraser was dotted with gold seekers.

Strikes followed at Horsefly, Quesnel Forks, Keithley Creek and Antler Creek. Then three major finds occurred in quick succession: at Williams Creek in February 1861; a mile away at Barkerville in the spring of 1862; another mile farther on at what was to become Camerontown in August 1862. Ten thousand miners rushed into the area. Suddenly the handful of missionaries, who had themselves only recently arrived in this far-west wilderness and were busy struggling to bring religion to an itinerant native population who spoke no English, found themselves faced with an entirely new challenge. Added to the huge population of First Nations people and the small group of white settlers was a new and steadily growing group of well-bred, well-educated adventurers. Many had travelled 6000 miles into the wilderness with only the most meagre supplies of food and household essentials, yet had included in their packs much-thumbed copies of Plutarch's *Lives*, Gibbon's *History of Rome*, Macaulay's *Essays*, and complete sets of Shakespeare.[53]

For most of these men this was a great adventure. Many were attracted to the challenge of pitting themselves against nature in an unexplored wilderness. All were confident that before many months had passed they would be well on the way to making their fortunes.

The discovery that the efforts of perhaps ninety-five miners in every hundred were resulting in little more than enough financial return to cover expenses, dismayed them but it didn't discourage them. They were convinced that it was just a matter of time until they would be among the percentage whose finds were significant. Until that should happen, they plunged into a carefree, self-indulgent life-style.

The gold towns became centres for gambling, drinking and prostitution. Of the 82 buildings in the original Barkerville, eighteen were gambling saloons with private rooms where "ladies" offered companionship. Antler, a nearby gold gown was described in 1862 as:

> . . . consisting of some sixty or seventy houses in two rows facing each other so as to form a street—unpaved and filthy dirty, though there was an attempt at a walk of plank—with the drinking and feeding saloons being most numerous.[54]

Such seemingly flagrant self-indulgence presented a challenge to the churches that they could not ignore. Despite the fact that there were as yet only about a dozen missionaries in this vast region west of the Rockies, the home churches encouraged those missionaries to journey north and reform the life-style of the miners.

They assumed the task would be relatively simple. Most of the men who had flocked to the gold fields were both intelligent and well educated. Surely it would take very little to encourage such men to change their life-style and refocus their attention on more essential things.

The character of the gold towns themselves encouraged this opinion. The same community that boasted eighteen saloons advertised the services of a dancing master and a professor of foreign languages. The same citizens whose working-day vocabulary was filled with profanity, attended evening elocution classes where the material studied was Bacon's "Essay on Vain Glory," Grey's "Ode on the Progress of Poetry," and Dickens's "Death of Little Nell." Admittedly, the gold towns condoned drinking, gambling and prostitution, but they also had Glee Clubs, choirs and a Debating Society. In 1864 a library and reading room were erected in Camerontown, and when the centre of population shifted to Barkerville, the library was moved there. An amateur theatre society was established and a theatre built. In 1869 the Pickwick Club was formed. Even politics had its place. Long before British Columbia became a province the residents of Williams

Creek celebrated Dominion Day by flying their own "Canadian flag"—a Canadian beaver surrounded by a wreath of maple leaves set in the centre of the British Ensign.[55]

It is perhaps just as well that no one realized ahead of time just how difficult converting the life-style of the miners was going to prove to be.

Living conditions in the gold towns were truly appalling. There were well-to-do citizens like John Bowron, whose comfortable two-storey home in Barkerville boasted fine china and a piano that had been carried all the way up the Cariboo Trail on men's backs. But most of the miners in the early years lived in unfurnished, unheated, uninsulated shacks in a climate where wintertime temperatures dropped to forty below zero and where snow banks reached eight or more feet in depth.

For seven or eight months each year they stood day after day from daybreak till dusk up to their knees in icy water, panning the creek beds. One of the greatest causes of infection and illness was what the miners called "gum-boot fever," fifty years later referred to as trench foot.

With a proper diet the risk of infection might have been minimized, but most of these men subsisted on ill-cooked rice and porridge. Fruit and vegetables were non-existent in the gold fields, and flour, eggs, bacon and coffee were priced out of reach.

For many, the optimism that had been so strong at the start of their adventure was gradually giving way to discouragement.

"What a fool I was to come on a fool's errand," a young prospector wrote from Antler Creek to his family in October 1862. "If you could only see the number of men there are around here, many brought to a state bordering on starvation. About 800 men are camped around Antler, and all the claims that are paying on the creek are three."[56]

Two ill-prepared adventurers arrived in Williams Creek just as the peak of the gold rush was passing. They had come without provisions, equipment, or money, believing the wild stories that were circulating that gold nuggets were to be found lying on the ground just waiting to be picked up. Discovering to their horror that gold did not lie on the surface but had to be worked for, they offered the wife of one of the town's busiest blacksmiths a third of the fortune they expected to make if she would grub-stake them. The blacksmith's wife agreed. Two years later the men returned with just one small nugget to show for twenty-four months of heavy labour, which they gave to their grub-staking partner.

Miners struggling against depression had no wish to give up the few things that gave them pleasure. Moreover, even if they had wanted to support the missionaries, they couldn't afford to. Most of them had all they could do just to hold off starvation. They had no money to donate towards the building of a church or the living expenses of a missionary.

The parent churches, however, did not seem to realize this. Urging their missionaries to travel north to the gold fields, they were confident the miners would welcome them and support them.

The first Man of God to arrive in the gold fields was Roman Catholic Father Charles Grandidier who held a service in Richfield in the summer of 1861. Grandidier was a shy man, torn with self-doubt. Unfortunately an egg-throwing incident at a service he had conducted as he was travelling north had shaken his confidence. Now he was intimidated by the profanity and lawlessness of the miners, and did not make a second visit.

That same summer of 1861 two Anglican clerics held services at Antler Creek, the Reverend Lunden Brown and the Reverend Christopher Knipe. They were two of the group of men Hills had brought to the Columbia region, and had come for a five-year term without any salary.

By July of 1862 the number of Anglican missionaries making regular visits to the area had increased to four: Knipe, with his headquarters at Van Winkle; John Sheepshanks, another unsalaried five-year volunteer, holding services at Antler; R. J. Dundas, who travelled in and out of Williams Creek; and Bishop George Hills, who began the first of what was to be a regular series of episcopal journeys through the gold fields.

At first the results of these missionary visits were minimal. Since there were no church buildings the clerics were forced to hold services in the gambling saloons which were the only large rooms available. While the missionaries struggled to hold the attention of the few listeners gathered at one end, the crowd of drinkers and gamblers made jokes and rude comments at the other, for most of them had no wish to be lectured. Drinking, gambling and prostitution provided the only escape that made their lives bearable.

During their first two years in the gold fields the missionaries met with constant ridicule and opposition. If they dared to criticize, the mining communities united against them. For weeks after Lunden Brown preached a particularly heated sermon condemning the "prevailing vice" of prostitution, not one single person attended any of his services in any of the gold centres.[57]

It is probable that Christopher Knipe's disillusionment and ultimate defection had their roots in this very first year of his term of service, for he admitted to Bishop Hills in May 1862 that the miners of Williams Creek had warned him not to criticize any of the faults he would find there, the gambling, the brawling, the swearing, or they would refuse to contribute anything at all towards his travel and living expenses.[58]

Another difficulty facing the missionaries was the northern climate and terrain.

> "Constantly I had to dismount, my horse being immovably fixed up to his belly in the bog," Hills writes in his journal of a trip from Van Winkle to Richfield in the spring of 1862. "Indeed, most of the way I led him, and was frequently over my knees in bog and water, and wet all through. Several times I fell over logs and once into a stream."

Summer was no improvement. In describing an evening meal during a visit to Antler that same summer, John Sheepshanks writes:

> There was a ceaseless hum in the apartment for it was literally brown with . . . thousands of mosquitoes. Each man wore his coat buttoned up, strings fastened round his cuffs and trousers, gauntlets on his hands, his hat on his head with a veil hanging down covering his face and neck. He would stick his fork into a piece of meat and pop it in under the veil as quickly as possible . . . Not a word was uttered. We were too beaten down and cowed by insects.[59]

The discomfort of the missionaries' own living conditions didn't help.

> "I lived at Camerontown in a small shanty some six by eight feet," Lunden Brown reported to the Columbia Mission on his return to England in 1864. "It was so situated that the creek occasionally overflowed into it, and I have gone home of a Sunday night to find it full of water with the planks of the floor, the stools, pans, etc. all floating about in a lively manner."

Had the results of their missionary labours been more encouraging, it might have been easier for these Men of God to put up with the hardships facing them. Early in 1863 John Sheepshanks was stopped on the street in Barkerville by a man and woman asking if he would marry them. All too few residents of the gold towns cared anything about the sanctity of the marriage ceremony and Sheepshanks was delighted. "Certainly" he told them, "if it is right, and after proper notice is given." At that the miner shuffled his feet in embarrassment. "W'al, y'understand," he blustered, "it's only to be for the season."[60]

For some the combination of discouragement, hardship and isolation was too much. "The mass of people were reckless and ungodly," Lunden Brown wrote to the missionary society in 1864, justifying his own early return to England. "To induce these people to listen to the Gospel it must be preached with great power . . . For myself, let me candidly own it, I have not succeeded."[61]

Yet despite all this, the presence of the missionaries gradually began to make itself felt in the mining communities. In the spring of 1863 Anglican John Sheepshanks constructed the first church. He paid five hundred dollars for a lot in Richfield and on it he built a tiny log cabin church. The windows were never paned and the inside furnishings were rough but it held a dozen or more worshippers. Later that year a Methodist church was constructed at Camerontown on land given to Methodist missionaries Ephriam Evans and Arthur Browning. It, too, was a tiny log cabin, never completely finished but usable for services. The following year Roman Catholic missionary Father McGuckin converted a small cabin at Richfield into another place suitable for holding church services.

That same year, 1864, the first Presbyterian minister arrived in Richfield, the Reverend Daniel Duff. Eager, perhaps, to make up for the fact that his church was three years behind the others in reaching the gold fields, Duff did not leave when fall came, but determined to be the first missionary to stay through the winter.

In his own words it was "a most lonely" time. However, the fault was partly his own. Admittedly the level of ethical behaviour in the gold fields deserved criticism. Brawls were common, prostitution was prevalent, and there was no observation of the Sabbath. But Duff seemed unable to do anything but criticize. In particular he attacked the saloons and the buxom, good-natured hurdy-gurdy girls who sang and danced there. It was probably this more than anything else that caused the miners to unite against him. The following spring he left Williams Creek for the Kootenays and did not return.

It was unfortunate that in his enthusiasm to reform the existing social pattern, Duff failed to see that for the first time there was developing a real need for the Men of God in the gold fields. The early euphoria evident in 1861 and 1862 was gone. Gradually, disillusionment had taken its place. And this disillusionment was now often tinged with hopelessness. Miners, who for two or three or even four years had, despite all their setbacks, continued to believe in that miracle "strike," had at last accepted the truth. But ironically, now that they were finally ready to give up and go home they could no longer do so, for they no longer had the funds or the health to undertake the long journey.

The Reverend A. C. Garrett, an Anglican who made his first visit to Richfield just as Duff was leaving, saw what Duff had failed to see. It was one of his reports that first alerted the church at home to the change that was occurring.

Thousands of dollars are expended here [Richfield] before any result is obtained, and in many instances without ever meeting with any reward. Still the success of a few is so dazzling that many men cannot resist the spell to try again and yet again. . . . The known gold fields are now, indisputably, rapidly approaching exhaustion. Unless something new can be discovered this season, next year will find the whole country in a miserable state of stagnation.[62]

Garrett's assessment of the situation was astute. During 1861 and 1862 the missionaries had gone into the gold fields mainly in the hope of instilling a sense of responsibility and self-control among the miners. Although the results of their efforts were minimal, they were confident that in time they would make an impact, for the gold towns were busy, thriving, culturally active communities. By 1864, however, the change was marked. The mining communities were no longer busy or thriving. For the first time the gold rush communities needed the influence and the leadership of the Men of God.

"In a ministerial point of view this is the most important place in British Columbia," Garrett's letter went on. . . . "But only a special type of man should be sent, one who is competent to command the respect and conciliate the good will of all classes."[63]

In 1864 as the aura of failure started spreading, into the disillusioned gold-rush community came John Fraser, the son of explorer and Hudson's Bay Factor Simon Fraser.

Born in 1833, John was the third youngest of Fraser's nine children. He was the family favourite, personable, friendly and intelligent. He did well at school, graduating as a certified engineer, and would probably have had little difficulty in finding suitable employment in England, but in 1862 Simon Fraser died. As was the case with many of the Hudson's Bay factors, partly as a result of unwise investments made on their behalf by the Hudson's Bay Company, Fraser had no savings or capital. All he had to leave to his eight surviving children was the large farm homestead.

It was hardly sufficient as a source of capital for eight livings, particularly when four of the family, Margery, Harriet, Roderick and James still lived on it. Accordingly, encouraged by the newspaper reports of the fortunes to be made in the gold-rush centres of the Cariboo, the Fraser family decided against parcelling the farm into eight pieces and mortgaged it instead, giving the money to John to take to the Canadian west to make their fortune. They were confident that John would succeed. With his mining engineering training, as well as his knowledge of surveying, they were convinced he would be better qualified than most of the prospectors in Canada's far west, and would have no difficulty recognizing a gold-bearing claim immediately and taking possession of it for his family.

Fraser arrived in the gold fields in the spring of 1864, bringing letters of introduction to Governor James Douglas both from Lord Monck, then Canada's Governor General, and from the Duke of Newcastle who was Secretary of State for the Colonies. Both letters included the statement that they had been written at the personal request of Sir John A. Macdonald.[64]

Fraser went first to Camerontown where he applied for and received his certificate as a "sworn surveyor." He then advertised his availability not only as a surveyor, but also as a qualified mining engineer. He was confident that there would be an immediate demand for his professional services, for most of the prospectors had no technical training of any kind.

By that spring of 1864, however, the prospectors who two or three years earlier might have welcomed the chance to hire him, could no longer afford to do so. It was unfortunate timing. Had Fraser come two years earlier, immediately after Simon Fraser's death, the situation might have been different. But now, particularly in Camerontown, the hectic growth period of the gold rush was over. A few years earlier Camerontown had been the scene of one of the most publicized strikes in gold-rush history, but most of the gold readily accessible through unsophisticated methods of sluicing and panning, had been mined out.

Hoping there might yet be some response to his advertising, Fraser waited in Camerontown till mid-summer, then he left and went to Barkerville.

He was an instant favourite. Within weeks he knew everyone and was included in every activity. He was elected president of the Literary Society, the Glee Club and the Library Association. Confident that this time he would have no trouble finding employment he again advertised his services, and waited.

Again there was no response.

Now, once again timing played a part. Had Fraser not waited so long in Camerontown, had he reached Barkerville while there were still three or four months of good working weather before winter, he might have set out to prospect on his own. Admittedly, he had no equipment, for he had expected to find employment in a professional capacity, but he had sufficient money to buy any equipment he needed. However, it was now late summer. In this fourth year of the gold rush the only areas still available where a newly arrived miner could stake a claim were miles from civilization. Had it been spring or even early summer Fraser would probably not have hesitated, but in a matter of weeks winter would set in. It made more sense now to wait until spring, he decided. Besides, life in Barkerville was pleasant.

It was also expensive. The chief sources of amusement were drinking and gambling. The basic necessities of food, lodging and clothing essential to survive a Barkerville winter were priced at many times their normal value. By spring the money Fraser's family had raised by mortgaging the family farm had all been used up.

Again Fraser looked without success for someone to hire him as an engineer or surveyor, and now the alternative of setting out to prospect on his own no longer existed, for he had no money left to buy equipment.

While he was still trying to decide what to do, the first spring mail arrived in Barkerville, bringing him two letters. The first was from his family, announcing that the mortgage they had taken out on the farm had been foreclosed. The second was from the girl he had been engaged to, telling him that she had decided not to wait any longer for him to return from the gold fields, and had married someone else.

Letters from Barkerville citizens Harry Jones and Robert Stevenson, a family friend of Fraser's whose home was within a dozen miles of the Fraser homestead, contain references to young Fraser's "severe depression."[65]

That spring a young miner eluded the friends who were taking turns staying with him and cut his throat with a kitchen knife. Historians disagree on whether or not that man was Fraser, but whether he was, or whether Fraser succumbed to depression and malnutrition, he died in Barkerville on May 20th, 1865 and is buried in the Barkerville cemetery. He was 32 years old. According to the report of his funeral in the *British Columbian* on June 1st, 1865, "His remains were borne to their last resting place by the largest concourse of friends ever before assembled in Cariboo for such a purpose."

Fraser was typical of hundreds of prospectors who flocked to Barkerville only to find their dreams turn into the worst kind of nightmare.

By 1865 heartbreak, disillusionment and despair were common. The need for more Men of God was great. But ironically, as the need for the missionaries grew more pronounced, the churches at home reduced their support for missionary work in the Canadian gold fields. The reason was a combination of reduced missionary giving at home and the limited response given to the missionaries' efforts by the miners during the gold-rush boom years of 1861, 1862 and 1863. As the level of available funds began to drop, it was decided that what little money there was should go to finance projects that were known to be successful.

From the summer of 1865 until August 1868 no Protestant missionary visited any of the gold towns, and the only Roman Catholic missionary to travel north stayed only a few weeks. Sheepshanks's Anglican log cabin church at Richfield, Ephriam Evans's Methodist log cabin at Cameron-town, and the cabin Father McGuckin had converted for Roman Catholic services at Richfield all stood empty.

Then in 1867 a group of Welsh miners under the leadership of Captain John Evans petitioned Cariboo Gold Commissioner W. G. Cox for a site at the north end of Barkerville. They used the site to build the Cambrian Hall, and began holding lay-conducted church services on Sundays. Some of the English miners asked to be allowed to hold services there as well and were given permission to use the hall on alternate Sunday evenings.

Attendance at the services was small, but the fact that even a few came seemed all the encouragement Evans needed. As the newly elected member for Cariboo West in the Colony of British Columbia Legislative Assembly, Evans now wrote an open letter to the editor of the *Cariboo Sentinel*, signing it only with his initials, J.E.

The letter began with a boast about the gradually steadying influence that seemed to be evident throughout the mining communities, and about the recent decision of the Hudson's Bay Company to close their stores on Sunday, which up until then had been the chief business day of the week. It then went on to criticize the church for no longer making any effort to provide services for "the masses that are approaching eternity as if the great aim of life is the gathering of gold and the spending of it."[66]

The letter attacked the Anglican Church specifically, accusing its missionaries of giving up their earlier missionary efforts just because the conditions in the gold fields could be sometimes uncomfortable. He called them "feather-bed soldiers of the cross," and criticized them for "indulging in good living and easy work in the lower country, while . . . in Barkerville hosts of men lounge along the streets with nothing open as an alternative but the saloon."

Two weeks later one of Hills's clergy published a letter in reply defending the Bishop, stating that he had made repeated efforts to raise funds for a resident clergyman in Barkerville but with no results.

Evans wrote again, first condemning Hills for having left his defence to one of his clergy instead of answering himself, then accusing him of discontinuing missionary visits to such places as Barkerville because he preferred to use the money on land speculation. Lastly he accused Hills of being a man of little faith, who did not follow the example of the Apostles whom he claimed to succeed but was afraid to take any steps into the unknown.[67]

It is unlikely there was any truth in the land speculation accusation, for Hills had consistently shown a conservative attitude in that area. Several times during 1860 and 1861 he had failed to act on opportunities to buy land in Victoria. In 1865 when John Sheepshanks was preparing to return to England and made Hills a gift of a large section of downtown Victoria property which might have made the Anglican Church in British Columbia self-supporting to this day, Hills promptly sold it.[68]

The accusation that Hills was a man of little faith was also unfair. But he could not allow the remarks to go unchallenged. He decided to accede to Evans's request and send a resident missionary to Barkerville.

The man he selected for the task was James Reynard, a deacon working at that time in an Indian mission in Victoria.

Reynard was ill suited for frontier life both physically and temperamentally. A thin, frail man, he had been plagued all his life by ill health, and had needed weeks to recover from the effects of his months-long sea voyage to Canada. Instead of being innovative, outgoing and self-reliant, qualities both A. C. Garrett and Lunden Brown had specified as essentials for anyone hoping to minister in the gold fields, Reynard was withdrawn and shy. His abilities lay almost exclusively in the areas of music and languages. In addition he had a wife and several small children to support, and the northern wilderness was singularly unsuited for either women or children.

Hills, however, saw Reynard's family situation as an added reason for selecting him. When some of his own clergy opposed the idea, arguing that starvation might be the result, Hills replied:

> The presence of a lady, though certain to suffer great hardship, would be of much value to such a community. Her presence with her children would be a pledge to the people that the clergyman proposed to settle down and cast his lot with them; hostages, as it were, to prove that his would be no mere summer visit.[69]

Protests were immediately forthcoming. On the morning of the day that Reynard and his family were scheduled to leave Victoria Judge Matthew Begbie wired, "They will starve. Wait one week. I write by mail." Later that same day a second telegram arrived signed by a number of prominent Victoria citizens urging Hills to await letters from several of them before making a final decision, but Hills refused to wait.

The following week Begbie's letter arrived, spelling out the difficulties and criticizing the five-hundred-pound annual stipend that Hills was offering.

> A family of four or five persons could not provide themselves with food and fire for five hundred pounds. Cordwood is very expensive, and in the winter a

lavish consumption is necessary for existence. Mr. Reynard and his family could not even support themselves with food and fire for five hundred pounds, without adding a farthing for clothes.

And where are he and his family to go? I have been making inquiries and cannot find a single house vacant or attainable in which a married woman and children could be expected to live.

How is the house to be furnished? . . . How are travelling expenses to be defrayed? When he comes, where will he preach? What will they do? Whither will they go? How can they either stay or return?[70]

In his private journal Hills admitted the difficulties Reynard would be facing, but he refused to alter his decision. "Better we should face the risk of starvation for one of our clergy," he wrote, "than that the charge of neglect should remain for our church."

In August 1868 Reynard and his family left Victoria and set out for Barkerville. "The difficulties facing me have hardly been overstated," he admitted to Bishop Hills in a letter shortly after his arrival in the gold town.

Since the only Anglican church building was Sheepshanks's cabin in Richfield, which could only hold a dozen people, Reynard began holding services in Penfold's Saloon. At the same time he launched an appeal for funds to build a proper church and also a rectory for himself and his family.

Despite the picture Evans had painted of the gold-town residents eagerly awaiting the arrival of a resident missionary, neither of Reynard's appeals received any support. Unskilled in any kind of carpentry, Reynard was forced to spend a portion of his meagre stipend to pay for a cabin to be built. "12 feet by 10, and the whole household living in it," he later described it.

He had been in Barkerville less than a month when on September 16th, 1868, fire broke out in Barry and Adler's Saloon. Before it finally burned itself out the entire town had been destroyed, including Penfold's Saloon where Reynard had been holding services.

"All my efforts and expenditures have been in vain" he wrote to the bishop. "All my lamps, benches, robes, books gone without a trace. Most people advise me to leave at once, but this I cannot, will not think of."

His cabin had escaped because it was situated a mile away at Richfield, but he knew he would have to raise funds somehow for a new church building. However, he delayed doing so, partly because of the rejection his first appeal had received, and partly because he wanted to give the residents of Barkerville time to recover from their own personal losses before asking them to contribute towards the construction of a church. A laudable but in this case questionable sentiment. He shouldn't have hesitated. While he was still pondering, a second missionary arrived in Barkerville, Methodist Thomas Derrick, who felt no reluctance whatever to ask the residents of the burned-out gold town to contribute funds for both a church and a rectory.

It was a quirk of fate that had kept Derrick from arriving in Barkerville before the fire, and losing all his church furnishings as Reynard had done. He was an exercise enthusiast and on his trip to Barkerville had made a habit of getting off the stagecoach once or twice each day and running ahead for two or three miles. He did this just a mile or two west of the Cache Creek junction where the road from Kamloops joins the Cariboo Trail. By mistake he took the turn to Kamloops. By the time he realized he was on the wrong road the stagecoach was miles away, for the driver refused to turn back for "anyone dumb enough to run when he could ride."[71]

The miners had ignored Reynard's appeal a month earlier, but now, perhaps because they found the outgoing Derrick more attractive, they contributed enough money to buy building materials for both a church and a rectory, and volunteered to help construct both of them. But still only a few attended services.

Part of the blame for this, and for the lack of support Reynard was receiving must fall on Captain John Evans. Having forced Hills into sending a missionary, he now ridiculed him. In a public statement he accused Reynard's services of being "so dry and formal that I feel very little edified when I get an opportunity to attend."[72]

In June of 1869 the Methodist church was officially opened. Determined not to be left behind, Reynard resolved that he would have some sort of Anglican church building available for use by Christmas at the latest. By this time he had managed to collect several small donations of money to which he added his own Christmas quarter's salary. It was money he could ill afford, but he had no choice, for he could not build the church himself and had to hire carpenters and pay them.

He engaged the two best carpenters available and paid them each ten dollars a day. Lumber cost ten cents a foot. Nails were twenty-five cents a pound. By the time carpenters Bruce and Mann had laid the foundation and framed the outer walls, Reynard had spent all his money. He could not even afford to have a roof put over the structure and the stains left by that first winter's snow are still visible on the walls. But the plans for the building included a small meeting room separated by a door from the main church building, and Reynard determined that this room at least would be ready in time for Christmas.

"I set to work by myself with my two lads for assistance," he reported to the Columbia Mission. "They are only little fellows, but they could hold one end of a board while I secured the other, and between us we finished the room in time."[73]

However, it seemed he was once again in for disappointment.

The Barkerville people at this time grieved me much. . . . Open ridicule is hard to bear. On Christmas day three persons attended service; on the following Sunday morning, two; that same evening, none. Now seemed the justification of all the condemners of my building at all, and of my building a church as a still more foolish thing.[74]

The report ended, however, with a statement of faith that could well be Reynard's personal motto and the motto of many of these early Men of God:

I am not afraid of poverty or of labour, but I am afraid of doing less than my all, or of offering to God that which costs me as little as possible.

Perhaps as a result of Evans's ridicule there were still only a small number of residents of Williams Creek who attended regular church services, and most of these preferred to go to Derrick's comfortably furnished church down the street. Reynard's congregations remained small, with the result that the offertory was not enough to cover the costs of holding services. Reynard had to dip into his own meagre funds to buy oil for the lamps, wood for the stove, and to replace the prayer books and service forms lost in the fire. It meant cutting down even more on his family's basic food and firewood.

At the start of his second winter Reynard determined to find a way to earn some extra money. He advertised in the *Cariboo Sentinel* offering his services as a private tutor in "Greek, Latin, English, Band, Chess, Euclid, Choir Music and History," for a fee of ten dollars per month. Despite the wide range of classes offered, he had few takers, perhaps because a Monsieur Deffis, who advertised himself as a Professor of Languages, was also offering lessons. The result was that during the winter of 1869-70 Reynard and his family came close to starvation.

"We live as cheaply as possible," he reported to the Columbia Mission in London. "Potatoes on Sundays by way of marking the Christian feast, and a cabbage on Christmas Day as a very especial delicacy. We tried more stringent economies than these but I was losing my memory and getting morbidly afraid of meeting people, and reduced to the merest melancholy. It's no use; if you take it out of yourself, you must put it in, and this is no country for banyon days or bread-fruit trees."[75]

It is surprising that Hills should not have attempted to send him additional funds or even moral support. He could not have assumed that the Barkerville mission was self-supporting, for he had Reynard's regular reports to refute such a belief. But Hills sent no further assistance, made no mention of Reynard's work in the diocesan reports he sent back to England, and launched no special appeals to help the Barkerville mission.

In May 1870 Reynard wrote him personally reporting on the winter he and his family had just managed to get through:

> We were poor, my Lord, and the cold made life all the harder. We were camped at nights round the fire in the most sheltered part of the house, the little ones crying from the cold.
>
> A bottle of Communion wine froze under my wife's pillow the night the baby was born . . . bringing to seven the number of persons living in a ten by twelve foot cottage . . . If the decrease of income be not made up my wife and children will have to leave before next winter. I cannot allow them to face another such time of hardship.[76]

The decrease in income he was referring to was caused by his having to use his own salary to help finance the construction of the church and to pay for service supplies.

Still Hills made no move to help.

Perhaps it was the contrast between Reynard's and Derrick's ministries that caused Hills's behaviour. Perhaps he saw Reynard as a poor advertisement for the Anglican Church, particularly when the Methodist minister was so popular and so much admired. Perhaps Hills saw Reynard's unpopularity as a reflection on his own abilities as a bishop.

What ever the reason, Hills's silence, his refusal to send any help or encouragement, combined with the severe cold, the inadequate food, and Reynard's own determination to work himself unstintingly, resulted in the breakdown of his health.

An accident that January further complicated matters. The winter was particularly severe even for Barkerville, and Reynard's firewood ran out. He had managed to buy a small additional supply the previous fall but it had been neither cut nor stacked, and lay almost a mile from his cabin, buried under four feet of snow.

> "Sleigh loads of good dry wood passed our door again and again," he wrote in his report to the Columbia Mission, "which made the tenth commandment a great difficulty. There was no help for it. I turned out in the bitter cold, mined under the snow and hauled a week's fuel home. I had boasted of my strength and health, and fearlessness of the rudest labour . . . but the last log I dragged up

the hill fell on my right hand, numb with cold, and broke the wrist. That day J. Reynard learnt how much physical endurance he is capable of. I persevered in the wood business till the logs were sawn and split and the house filled with fuel, then I collapsed upon my pain."[77]

Five months later Reynard's wrist was still so swollen it was impossible for him to hold a pen. What worried him most was that he had again advertised his services as a tutor for the fall of 1870, this time for $7.50 a week, and had at last received some response. Several music students wished to study with him. He needed the money badly as a source of extra income, but his fingers were too swollen to play the piano. However, as he later explained to the Columbia Mission, he "fell back on the violin and managed to scrape through."

In June 1870 Reynard wrote to the Columbia Mission, explaining that his church was not yet finished and that services were still being held in the attached meeting room. He asked for six hundred dollars to complete the building. No money was forthcoming, so Reynard appealed once again to the mining community. As before his appeal was ignored.

Inured by this time to rejection, Reynard decided to disregard the expense and hired carpenters to complete the building. By the end of the summer the work was finished, and on September 18, 1870, Reynard's dream was realized and St. Saviour's Church was officially opened. The cost was $4,240, more than twice the cost of the Methodist church, primarily because Reynard had been unable to obtain any volunteer labour. But the professional workmanship was not wasted, for the original church is still standing a century and a quarter later and is still in regular use for Sunday services.

From the outset Reynard insisted that he was not building a church but a "miniature cathedral," and this is exactly what he built. The original stained-glass windows are still in place today, as are the original pews hewn from the pine trees that covered the local hills. The original stove is also unchanged. The Bishops's Chair made of English oak and inlaid with ebony and white ivory which sits in the chancel is the one Reynard brought to Barkerville in 1870.

By the start of another winter Reynard was ill. By the following spring he could no longer conduct services. He requested permission to resign, and four years later at the age of 45 was dead of a brain tumor.

Once again the gold fields were without a minister, for Derrick had left some months earlier. But the Men of God had done their job. The gold rush was over. The population of Barkerville, Richfield and Camerontown which had exceeded two thousand in 1862, now nine years later numbered less than two hundred.

Even without a resident minister, Reynard's "miniature cathedral" continued to serve as a centre of worship for the area. It has continued to serve from that time right up to the present.

Chapter 5

BRIDESHIPS: IT SEEMED A
GOOD IDEA AT THE TIME

O NE OF THE FIRST Columbia Mission clerics to make a
trek north into the gold fields was the Reverend
Lunden Brown. In the spring of 1861 he travelled up the Cariboo Trail,
intending to hold services wherever he found pockets of population, and
hoping to influence the lifestyle of the miners.

He held services, but the miners did not attend. They were not inter-
ested. Nor would they listen to any attempts on his part to reform their life-
style.

Brown based his opinion on more than one visit to the area. During the
summer of 1861 and the spring of 1862 he made several more trips to
Richfield, Antler and Keithley Creek. On each successive visit he became
more upset. It seemed to him the extent of the lawlessness and self-
indulgence was not improving but deteriorating. As more gold seekers
flooded into the area the incidence of gambling, prostitution and immoral-
ity steadily increased.

What bothered Brown more than the gambling and the drunkenness
was the widespread prostitution. He referred to it as the "prevailing vice."
The women involved were almost exclusively First Nations, some as young
as nine or ten years of age. Many were "sold" with hardly a moment's
hesitation if the price offered by the miner was high enough.

Brown was determined to try to change things. He reasoned that if the
miners could be provided with wives there would be no further need for
prostitution. Moreover, if they had wives, they would soon have children
and family responsibilities, which should also solve the problems of gambling and drunkenness. Accordingly he decided to approach church leaders

in England and propose a scheme for bringing several shiploads of brides to the western Canadian gold fields.

It was not an original scheme. Between 1832 and 1836 more than 3000 British women had successfully emigrated to Australia on sixteen different ships.[78] Various British charitable organizations had organized and supported these schemes, apparently without any major problems, selecting the women from various orphanages or workhouses.

Undoubtedly the success of these earlier schemes was one reason for the favourable response Brown's proposal received, but there were other reasons as well. One was the marked increase of unemployed, unskilled women that had resulted after the opening in 1848 of Britain's first secondary schools for women. Suddenly hundreds of women who had formerly held jobs as nannies, teachers and governesses were out of work, replaced by the better-trained graduates of the new secondary schools.

By the early 1860s the situation had become desperate. In 1862 an advertisement appeared in *The Times* inviting applications for a position as a nursery governess. No secondary school education would be required, the notice stated. The salary cited was "fifteen pounds per year maximum." More than 450 women applied.[79]

Another reason Brown's suggestion met with approval was the steadily increasing burden of taxation falling on the people of Britain to support the growing number of orphanages and workhouses. All the existing institutions were overcrowded. More were needed each year. Many people felt that any scheme that promised to relieve the situation by sending some of the women to a new life in a new land was well worth supporting.

Lunden Brown put his proposal in writing and sent it to John Garrett in London, commissary for Bishop Hills. Garrett presented it to the annual meeting of the Columbia Mission in February, 1862.

> "The Cariboo country has been shown to be one of the richest gold regions in the world," Brown's report read. "The mines were discovered only last winter. This summer 2000 men have been at work there, and next summer we anticipate an immigration of at least 10,000, perhaps more . . .
>
> "The cure for what, if let alone, will ultimately ruin religion and morals in this fine country, is an emigration of white women from Great Britain. Dozens of men have told me they would gladly marry if they could. I was speaking one evening on the subject of the dearth of females, and mentioned my intention of writing to beg that a plan of emigration may be set on foot, whereupon one member of the company immediately exclaimed, 'Then sir, I pre-empt a wife.' Then another, and another, and all round the circle exclaimed the same."[80]

Brown's letter went on to compare the situation in England where there were 600,000 more women than men to the situation in the Cariboo where there were almost no white women and certainly no unattached ones. He outlined a plan for sending the "brides" by steamship, and for starting an emigration fund to pay their way. He conceded that only girls of lower-class upbringing should be sent in order that Britain should not be robbed of anyone who would be a potential "leading" citizen.

Brown, himself, was held in high regard by the membership of the Columbia Mission. He had a reputation for being scholarly and serious-minded, and his concern for the new colony had been shown by two treatises he had written documenting the political, social and economic situation in Canada's far west, and commenting candidly on the lawless-ness and moral laxity that existed in the new colony. A year later he was pressured by the British colonial secretary into softening his comments. If he didn't the treatises would be refused publication, the colonial secretary threatened, and Brown finally backed down, but his real views were well known.

Immediate support for Brown's brideship scheme came from the Bishop of Oxford. Stating first that Brown's plan would provide the girls who were chosen with an opportunity for patriotism and self-sacrifice which they would probably never encounter again, the bishop went on to say that they would "thank us for having given them the opportunity of serving their country, their race, and their God."[81]

With this endorsement, Brown's proposal was passed enthusiastically. The Columbia Emigration Society was formed, and a committee was empowered to select suitable girls from orphanages and workhouses in Britain to go to the gold fields. It was agreed that these girls should be as young as possible, perhaps even thirteen or fourteen, and that they should be "placed in domestic service until they received the anticipated offers of marriage."[82]

The moment the plan was made public the committee received a flood of applications. One woman wrote begging to be allowed to volunteer together with her five daughters, for her clergyman husband had died and they were left with no means of support.[83]

There were so many such requests that Garrett wrote an open letter to *The Times* clarifying the Society's position. He admitted that the situation for many middle-class women was just as serious as it was for the lower-class ones, for ". . . such women cannot enter our English kitchens, not from an unwillingness to work but because they have not learned that particular business. And if a benevolent lady should try one of them either as a waiting maid or as a housemaid there is an immediate conspiracy among the professional servants against the intruder."[84] He sympathized with the middle-class women who were begging to be allowed to volunteer, but explained that it was the Society's firm intention to send only lower-class untrained girls.

Instead of stopping the requests, Garrett's letter seemed to bring more of them, and at last the Columbia Emigration Society agreed to compromise and accept a certain percentage of middle-class women along with the orphanage and workhouse girls.

The first group numbered just twenty, all mature women chosen from the hundreds of applications the committee had received. They left England on April 17, 1862, just seven weeks after Brown's proposal had been presented.

Unfortunately, either because of the haste with which this first group was dispatched, or because of the inexperience of the committee, adequate preparations were not made for the women's reception. No notice was sent to church or civic officials notifying them of the women's arrival. As a result there is no record that the citizens of Victoria, New Westminster or Esquimalt were aware that the women had landed. The fact that none of them made any attempt to draw herself to the attention of the authorities suggests that all twenty must have readily found a niche for themselves, or decided against being a miner's bride.

Two months later a second contingent of women left London on board Her Majesty's ship *Tynemouth*. According to *The Times* the ship was supposed to leave the London docks "punctually on the 24th of May" but left instead on June 9. One-hundred-and-one days later on September 17th, 1862, they docked at Esquimalt Harbour. There were sixty women this time. Forty were girls between 13 and 16 years of age chosen from British orphanages. They had only a rudimentary education, no vocational skills, and were completely dependent on the church-run Society that was sponsoring them. The other twenty were mature middle-class women between 20 and 35 years of age, members of the newly formed British Female Middle-Class Emigration Society (FMCES). Most of these women were either teachers or governesses, whose positions in England had been lost to the graduates of the new secondary schools.

Unable to find work at home, these women were drawn to the idea of emigrating to Canada's far west by reports from government and church leaders of the need for such services there. The scarcity of good nannies and governesses, particularly throughout the area of Columbia, had been a major argument used by Bishop George Hills two years earlier in his appeal to Baroness Angela Burdett-Coutts for funds to build a good girls' school in Victoria. With the announcement by the Anglican Church of Brown's "brideship" scheme, many FMCES women applied to come along, realizing that travelling under the aegis of the church would give them both security and respectability in an era when women didn't travel half-way around the world unescorted.

From the outset they made it clear that they did not intend to be "brides." They wished to travel with the Columbia Mission party, but they considered themselves independent, for most of them were prepared to pay their own passage, and those who couldn't, contracted to reimburse the FMCES as soon as they were settled in positions in Canada.

The Columbia Mission was happy to have them, for Brown's scheme to bring order to the mining communities by an influx of marriageable women could only benefit by an influx of teachers and governesses as well. Accordingly they agreed that some twenty FMCES teachers and governesses would join the Columbia Mission group on board the *Tynemouth*.

Almost as soon as the voyage was underway, some of the FMCES group were regretting their decision to join the Columbia Mission party. The quarters allotted to the sixty girls and women were well below the water line in the lowest section of the vessel. The cabins were grossly overcrowded, inadequately lit, unventilated and constantly damp. During the hundred-and-one-day voyage, with the exception of brief daily airings when they were allowed to go up on deck in small rigidly supervised groups, the girls and women spent their time in the damp, semi-dark conditions of their steerage compartments. They were not even allowed off ship during the two stops it made during the course of the three-month journey, once for thirteen days in the Falkland Islands and later for two days in San Francisco. While all the other passengers went ashore and wrote diary records of their delight at tasting fresh fruit and milk and meat after weeks of stale salt rations, the sixty women bound for the gold fields were forbidden to leave their quarters.

The excessive restraint was in reaction to the treatment received by two groups of girls sent to Australia some years earlier. Two hundred single women travelling in 1835 on board the *James Pattison*, and 200 more travelling some years later aboard the *Indian*, had not been kept under adequate supervision and apparently had been subjected to drunken attacks by both passengers and crew. The matter was sufficiently newsworthy to have been discussed in the British parliament in February 1850[85] and was still remembered. The Columbia Mission Emigration Society was determined the same thing would not happen again. They employed a staff of three to look after the sixty women — the Reverend William Richard Scott, his wife, Helen, and Mrs. James Robb — and asked that one of the three should have the girls under supervision at all times.

Round-the-clock supervision was not easy to arrange, however, for the Scotts had two young children of their own to look after, and Mrs. Robb was accompanied by her daughter and two small grandchildren. It was plain that the only way to effectively supervise the girls of the Columbia Mission group was to keep them rigidly segregated from the other passengers.

Even without the restrictions placed on the group by the Scotts and Mrs. Robb, the trip would still have been terrible, for the *Tynemouth* was ill suited for carrying passengers. It had been selected because that particular shipping line had an association with the Anglican Church, but even Bishop Hills quipped privately that the initials of the line's owner, W. S. Lind really stood for Worst Steamship Line. Some months later he admitted that the chief magistrate in Esquimalt, Captain Franklyn, and Captain Pike who was master of a sister vessel HMS *Devastation*, had both openly condemned the conditions that existed on board the *Tynemouth*. "Cleanliness was not sufficiently attended to . . . There was not authority enough on the ship . . . The Captain was set at defiance and had not coercive power enough to preserve discipline."[86]

The journey was made even worse by the weather. Almost immediately a severe storm struck, washing overboard the cow and several pigs that had been penned on deck and intended to be a source of fresh meat during the voyage. The storm was so severe that one of the first-class passengers describes the ship in his diary as a "floating hospital."[87]

The *Tynemouth* was also meagrely provisioned. Before the ship set sail every passenger was required to sign a contract agreeing to a weekly food allotment.[88] It consisted of:

5½ lb. biscuit	½ lb. rice
1 lb. preserved meat	1 lb. raw sugar
½ lb. soup and Bouilli	1½ lb. tea
1 lb. mess pork	3½ lb. coffee
1½ lb. Indian Beef	6 oz. butter
½ lb. salt fish	2 oz. salt
2 lb. flour	½ oz. mustard
1 lb. oatmeal	¼ oz. pepper
6 oz. suet	1 gill vinegar
½ lb. raisins & currents	6 oz. lime juice
⅔ pint peas	½ lb. preserved potato

The contract included the stipulation that if fresh meat was issued, the regular allotments of flour, rice, raisins, peas, suet and vinegar would be discontinued.

For the group travelling under the aegis of the Columbia Emigration Society the situation was even worse, for the steamship line refused to allow the ship's crew to cook for third-class passengers. Their weekly rations were delivered in bulk to their below-decks compartments, and it was their responsibility to have one of their members take the food each day to the galley and coerce the cook into preparing it.

With three hundred other passengers and crew to prepare meals for, the cook seldom agreed. Nor would he agree to allow any of the third-class passengers to cook for themselves in his galley. The result was that the girls had to rely on having their food prepared in large quantities at those rare times when the cook was not busy, then stored and eaten cold for perhaps several days.

As the trip continued the conditions in the below-decks compartments became more and more unbearable. The rough weather, lack of ventilation and absence of washing facilities resulted in almost constant sickness for everyone. Shortly before the Falkland Islands were reached one of the girls, Elizabeth Buchanan, died.

At last at 8 p.m. on September 17th, 1862, the *Tynemouth* reached Esquimalt Harbour where tugs were waiting to convey the passengers to Victoria. Eagerly they disembarked—all except the Columbia Emigration Society group, who remained in their below-decks quarters for two more days.

Scores of male citizens swarmed onto the dock and attempted to board the vessel according to the report in the Victoria *Colonist*, but harbour officials ordered them away.

Finally on September 19th, following such reports in the British *Colonist* as "We are highly pleased with the appearance of the 'invoice' and believe they will give a good account of themselves," the girls were taken off the *Tynemouth* by the tugboat *Forward* and transported to Victoria. A sign in a downtown clothing store shouted, "The girls have arrived! Now is your chance to get a fine suit of clothes to make a respectable appearance."[89]

They were put ashore at James Bay where the dock was lined with more than 300 waiting men, for all Victoria businesses had been closed for the occasion. Two by two the girls were marched up the quay to the Parliament Buildings where each was handed a bucket of soapy water. As the crowd watched they were ordered to wash as much of themselves as possible, and the clothes that had suffered so much from absence of laundering during the voyage.

Some of the girls became hysterical. Many were sick. All were homesick and frightened, suffering from malnutrition and lack of exercise. To have to tidy themselves under the ogling scrutiny of hundreds of males was a terrifying experience. Only after completing their washing were the girls allowed to continue their two-by-two parade along the length of the main street to the Marine Barracks where they were to be housed until it was determined exactly where each was to be sent.

Not all reached the Marine Barracks. One girl was stopped by a gold miner who had been living near Sooke. In a hurried whisper he explained that he had walked most of the night in order to get to Victoria on the chance of being fortunate enough to get one of the girls, and begged her to marry him. The girl let go of the hand of the partner with whom she had been walking and with one quick glance at Mrs. Robb, disappeared into the crowd. They were officially married three days later.[90]

Another girl not disappointed by her reception was orphan Sophia Shaw who had spent her whole life in one orphanage or another. From the moment of her arrival in Victoria Sophia caught the attention of a gold miner. He proposed. Before Sophia had even finished accepting, the miner reached into his pocket and drew out $2,000 in cash and gave it to her with instructions to buy some nice clothes with it before the wedding.[91]

On arriving at the Marine Barracks the new arrivals were officially greeted by two committees. One was the official reception committee made up of many of Victoria's leading citizens: Captain Verney, Mr. Graham, J. C. Davie, Gilbert Sproat, Robert Burnaby, the Reverend Edward Cridge, Dr. W. F. Tolmie, and Archdeacon Wright.[92]

The second committee consisted of women from Christ Church, including Mrs. Cridge, Mrs. James Douglas, Mrs. Nurries Margarets, Mrs. Alston, Mrs. Arthur Hillows, Mrs. Rhodes, Mrs. Trutch, and Mrs. R. Woods. It was this group who had arranged for the girls to be billeted at the Marine Barracks.[93] They now took control of arranging where the girls should go.

They divided them into two groups. Those aged fifteen or older were to be offered immediately as brides, and would be housed at the Marine Barracks until they had been proposed to. The fourteen-year-olds and the single thirteen-year-old in the group were to be placed in domestic service for at least a year, perhaps a little longer, until they were ready for matrimony. The salary for their domestic service was set at twenty or twenty-five dollars per month with room and board provided. Future employers were also to be charged an initial ten-dollar fee payable to the Women's Committee to help defray expenses and to ensure that no irresponsible persons should apply.

The committee made no attempt to pressure the FMCES women. Despite the fact that the demand for "brides" exceeded by far the number of girls in the group who were of marriageable age, they respected the wishes of the older women to work as teachers and governesses, and agreed that they could use the Marine Barracks as their headquarters until they found suitable positions.

Placement of the girls who were to be brides took little time to arrange. Among those whose marriages are recorded in *The Colonist* are Minnie Gillan, Emma Quinn, Jane Ogilvie, Mary Cooper, sisters Augusta and Emily Morris, Emily Abington, Mary Chase, Julia Hurst, Sarah Baylis, Mary Evans, sisters Isobel and Francis Curtis, Mary MacDonald, and a short time later after working some time in domestic service, Jane Saunders.[94]

Placing the younger girls satisfactorily in domestic service was sometimes not achieved as quickly as placing the brides. Sometimes the homes to which girls were sent did not prove satisfactory, as was the case with the single thirteen-year-old in the group.

She had been spoken for months earlier by Mrs. Mary Moody, wife of Colonel Richard Moody, officer commanding the Royal Engineers in New Westminster. Mrs. Moody was a leading figure in New Westminster society and the mother of five children. When she learned of the brideship plan she specifically asked to have the youngest girl in the group sent to work for her as a junior housemaid, so that after going to the trouble of training her, she would be guaranteed at least two or three years of service. But within days of the girl being sent to New Westminster, Mrs. Moody sent her back, complaining that she was "too young, too small, and incapable of sewing."[95]

The teachers and governesses of the FMCES group, meanwhile, were meeting with little success in their search for employment. It seemed the need for teachers and governesses in this far-west region was not as great as had been suggested. Long after almost all the younger girls had been placed either as brides or as housemaids, well over half the older women still waited at the Marine Barracks. Gradually they accepted the fact that they would have to settle for a more menial type of employment.

Among the women on board the *Tynemouth* were Charlotte and Louisa Townsend. They were of upper-middle-class parentage and had even brought with them to Canada a sewing machine and a trunk of pretty clothes. When they had set out they fully expected to find work as governesses, but had to settle instead for being "companions."

"From the moment of landing I was disappointed," Louisa admitted years later. "So was my sister. . . . I used to cry myself to sleep every night . . . though they kept Chinese help, there were tasks given me to do which were distasteful." [96]

Whether or not Lunden Brown's plan can be termed successful is open to debate, but it had an impact on the development of this new region. Granted, not many of the "brides" reached their intended destination in the gold fields, but they did reach the far west where they married and raised families. As for the FMCES group, many of them made a significant contribution. Florence Wilson is an example.

Born of middle-class parents and possessed of a remarkably good education by nineteenth-century standards, Florence Wilson had planned from the outset to be neither a gold-rush bride nor a governess, but a businesswoman. Having paid her own fare on board the *Tynemouth*, she was under no obligation to remain with the group when the ship docked in Esquimalt, but proceeded directly to Victoria with the rest of the regular passengers. Once there, she set herself up in business in downtown Victoria as the manageress of a book and stationery store.

Eighteen months later her profits were enough to enable her to move to Barkerville where, using her own books together with the donated library of Barkerville citizen John Bowron, she set up the gold field's first public library.

A third contingent of brides for the miners arrived in Victoria on January 12, 1863, on board the *Robert Lowe*. This time there were thirty-six girls in the group, mostly factory workers from Lancashire. They suffered none of the discomfort that the *Tynemouth* girls had suffered and their arrival was vastly different.

"We hope the committee in charge will make better arrangements for their landing than that in the case of the *Tynemouth*," an editorial in the Victoria *Colonist* urged just a few days before the *Robert Lowe* was due to dock. "There is not the slightest necessity for any parade. . . . We cannot conceive of anything more heartless or ill-conceived than to have poor young strangers, we don't care of what sex, subjected to the rude gaze of a motley crowd of roughs."

The editorial had the desired effect. There was no public display when the girls were brought ashore. They were met by the reception committee and lodged temporarily in the Marine Barracks as the earlier group had been. Within days all those of marriageable age had received at least one proposal, but the younger ones destined for domestic service again found themselves not so fortunate. Many were dismissed from their first and even their second placings because of their inexperience. One girl, Sarah Marsden, according to a note in Bishop Hills's journal, was dismissed "for being too religious." On arriving at her new position she had asked if she could have time off to attend church on Sunday and had been fired immediately.

This third group of "brides" was the last one to be sent to Canada's far west by the Columbia Mission Emigration Society, but the scheme had served a useful purpose. It may not have solved the problem of prostitution in the gold fields which it had been intended to solve, but it did bring more than a hundred women into the region at a time when women were badly needed. In addition, it served as a prototype for several later emigration schemes which were established over the next half century.

Chapter 6

EDUCATION:
SOME PLUSES AND SOME MINUSES

O NE AREA in which the influence of the early missionaries was particularly significant was that of educa-
tion. The Men of God were responsible to a great extent for shaping the
direction that education would take in this western region for the next half
century.

As early as 1824 Hudson's Bay Governor George Simpson recognized
the need for some form of educational institutions.

> "Had a long interview with Eight Chiefs belonging to the Flat Head,
> Coutonais, Spokan and other tribes who assembled here for the purpose of
> seeing me," he noted in his Journal. "The Spokan and Flat Head Chiefs put a
> Son each under my care to be Educated at the Missionary Society School, Red
> River, and all the Chiefs joined in a most earnest request that a . . . religious
> instructor should be placed among them."[97]

To this same end he brought Herbert Beaver to Fort Vancouver in 1836
to start a school for fort children.

In 1841, Simpson took up the cause again. In a letter to London he
urged:

> The gentlemen connected with the fur trade on this side of the mountains
> finding it inconvenient to send their children either to Europe or Red River
> Settlement for the benefit of education, are anxious that a boys' and girls' school
> should be established.[98]

He went on to suggest that the Company might "afford passage free of
charge to the teachers and to two female servants . . . provide board and
lodging . . . with salaries of one hundred pounds per year on five year
appointments."

The need for good schools in this far-west area was very real. If the boys had to go to Red River for their education, as did the three sons of Chief Factor Archie McDonald and his wife, their families did not see them again for five years.

The choice of Robert John Staines as the second Hudson's Bay chaplain was made because Staines was a schoolteacher.

Staines, however, was narrow-minded and bigoted. He objected to having to teach the fort children in his school, for they were the offspring of "fur-trade marriages." He believed himself to be a teacher of considerable ability. It was a waste of his time teaching children for whom the future offered little hope of advancement.

This was an attitude that was widely held. The problem facing the children of fur-trade marriages is pointed up in an anecdote historian W. L. Morton tells about Hudson's Bay Chief Factor Alexander Ross. Ross had married an Okanagan chief's daughter, a woman of charm and intelligence, but because she was Indian, their son was treated with disdain and discrimination. Ross was determined his son would have a fair chance, and finally decided to send him to the University of Toronto for a proper education. Several years later when Ross learned that his son had just been awarded the University of Toronto Gold Medal in classics, he paced the floor for a minute in silent satisfaction, then burst out delightedly, "And what will they think of the *brulés* now?"[99]

Staines, however, had no intention of wasting his time. He began advertising throughout the Pacific region for other students to attend his school. He claimed his school would be for the "sons and daughters of gentlemen, offering instruction in all gentlemanly subjects including Latin."

The advertisement caught attention. A good school was something upper-class parents in Victoria, Vancouver, New Westminster and Esquimalt had been desperately wanting. Before long Staines's school had attracted a sizable enrolment.

It is perhaps just as well that no girls registered, for discipline in Staines's classroom was strict, and living conditions at the school were spartan. Breakfasts and suppers consisted solely of "bread and treacle and clear tea." In the crowded dormitories each boy was given only one thin blanket to protect him from weather that often saw the water freeze solid in the wash jugs at the foot of the beds. Of even greater consequence for some of the pupils was the fact that anyone who managed by strict self-denial to save a crust of bread from dinner for a bedtime treat invariably discovered that "the rats had eaten it."[100]

In addition to the spartan living conditions and the excessive discipline, the academic program at Staines's school did not measure up to his advertisement. The result was a steady decrease in numbers of pupils. Just before the end of Staines's tenure the school closed entirely.

For the next few years there was no school in the far-west area. Then in 1858 Bishop Modeste Demers, during a visit to Quebec, persuaded the Mother House of the Sisters of St. Anne at Lachine to send out four nuns to start a school for Roman Catholic children.

In January 1860, Bishop George Hills arrived in Victoria and immediately set to work to establish a Protestant school. His particular concern was that it should have high academic standards.

"I am anxious to find a good man to take the headship of a Collegiate institution," he wrote home to England in March of 1860, ". . . a man of high calibre." [101] He added that the case was urgent.

Hills found the man he was looking for in the Reverend Charles T. Woods. He found several other teachers as well, all English clerics and all well grounded in classical literature, history, Latin and Greek. By June 1860 the Boys' Collegiate School was in operation.

Not only was Hills concerned that his school meet high academic standards, he was equally concerned that it meet the church's religious standards. In October 1860 when the Collegiate School was just getting started several influential Jewish families applied for admission for their sons. A total of twelve boys were involved, which would have made a significant difference to the fledgeling school's financial situation. Hills, however would not agree to enrol them, for their parents wanted the boys to be excused from attending Bible study.

Apparently Charles Woods was just as harsh a disciplinarian as Staines had been. Letters from some of his pupils attest to this. When Woods was made Archdeacon of Victoria and left the school to take up his diocesan duties, his students were instructed to write him a letter of congratulation. After several weeks' delay they finally complied, but couldn't resist ending with the comment, "We still respect you, even those of us too young to forego the wholesome discipline of the cane." [102] However, any dislike expressed by the students for the school or its headmaster was not shared by the missionaries. During the first twenty years of the school's life more than half the number of enthusiastic Anglican missionaries who came to the Canadian far west fired with zeal, sooner or later abandoned their mission stations and joined the staff of the Boy's Collegiate School. [103]

Having successfully launched his boys' school, Hills now appealed to his benefactress, Angela Burdett-Coutts, for financial support for a "female institution."

> I mentioned in a former letter my anxiety about the education of girls of the upper and middle classes. Governesses cannot be had, nor could they be retained by private families on account of the scarcity of the sex. My desire is to form a female Collegiate school . . . Rome has this at present altogether in hand.[104]

Miss Burdett-Coutts did not ignore the appeal. She accepted responsibility for the full endowment, and by September 1860 a girls' school was opened, appropriately named Angela College. Its staff had certificates in music, drawing and languages, and the graduates of Angela College were as polished in social graces as the graduates of any finishing school in Britain.

The need for an educational program for the Indian children now became a prime consideration. Not only the Columbia Mission clerics but the Roman Catholic missionaries as well were finding themselves severely hampered in their efforts to teach religion to the native people when none of the Indian tribes spoke any English. Accordingly it was decided to teach English to the children and hope that through them the entire Indian population could eventually be reached.

The first schools established for this purpose were casual day schools to which the native children came for several hours each day to learn sufficient English that they could be instructed in Christian principles and taught how to join in the worship services of the church. The problem however, was that most of the children did not stay long enough to learn more than just a few phrases. The native people moved with the seasons and with the game, and took their children with them. It was not unusual for a child to attend school faithfully for three weeks, then not be seen again for a year.

This was the reason that the idea of residential schools was first introduced. The schools did succeed in overcoming the immediate problems of an itinerant student body and no single common language, but they also caused immeasurable suffering and hardship for the native pupils. Cut off from their own life-style, these children were forced to accept a life-style and value system that was completely foreign to anything they had known before. Accustomed to eating once a day and sleeping when they were tired, these children were suddenly expected to be hungry at four-hour intervals and fall asleep only after the ringing of a bell. Where before they had lived out of doors and planned their activities to match the seasons, they were suddenly forced into a fixed monotonous daily schedule. Casual, comfortable clothes were replaced by heavy uniforms. Natural foods gave way to a diet of white bread and porridge that took them months to adjust to. The Methodist Church School at Kitimat, for example, discovered that the lethargy and depression of its students was directly linked to the absence in their diet of the sea-salt which they had been used to, and introduced sea-salt candy to remedy it.[105] Most other schools, however, expected porridge, baked beans and white bread to be readily acceptable.

There were more basic problems even than these. The children brought together in the schools belonged to as many as thirty different tribes, each speaking a different language and holding a different ranking within the social system. Children of the Haida or Tsimshian, for instance, were considered to merit greater respect than children from less important tribes. Children belonging to what the others considered "slave tribes" were expected to wait on their betters.[106]

The Residential Schools could not function with such class discrimination. Each child no matter what his parentage was expected to take his or her turn waiting on tables, helping in the kitchen, or working in the school's vegetable garden. The Crosby Home in Port Simpson, for example, was suddenly upended when the usually well-disciplined pupils began arriving up to an hour late for lessons and meals. The reason, it was finally revealed, was the admission of a new pupil—a girl who was a full-blooded princess in her own tribe. Unused to having to wait on herself she was demanding that the other girls help her dress, tidy her bed, and look after her clothes before starting to do the same things for themselves.

In order to avoid this sort of thing the Residential Schools set about deliberately distancing their pupils from their native background. Visits home were discouraged as were visits by parents to the schools. Native customs were not allowed, nor was the speaking of any native language. Those breaking the rules were severely punished. It was felt that such measures were necessary in order to have the pupils come together as a homogeneous group, but the effects were quite different from what the church had envisaged or intended. Rather than facilitating the integration of the Indian children into western society these measures set in motion a cycle of destruction. The denial of any recognition of native customs and the weaning of the children away from their family ties developed in them a sense of inferiority concerning their own culture which is only now being reversed.

The insistence that every child must speak English and only English was perhaps the most damaging rule of all. Not only did it alienate the children from their parents who spoke no English, but for the first year of their schooling when they were faced with having to adjust to so many shattering changes, it isolated them even from each other. No wonder so many of them risked the usual punishment of having their mouths taped, or being denied dinner, or enduring a day and a night in isolation in the tiny "cell" each school maintained when the need to communicate with someone in their own language was too great for them to bear.

✝

With the opening of Angela College a few months after the Boys' Collegiate School was established, in addition to the Roman Catholic school which had been in operation since 1858 under the direction of the Sisters from Lachine, education was available for both the sons and the daughters of upper-class white residents. The Indian Residential Schools, on the other hand, were initially only for boys. It was not until late in the 1870s that the first girls' school for native students was established, the Crosby Home in Port Simpson.

Funded by the Wesleyan Missionary Society, and established by missionary Thomas Crosby and his wife, Emma, the Crosby Home, like Angela College, had as its objective the preparation of its pupils for future lives as wives and homemakers. But unlike Angela College, the Crosby Home did not concentrate on instruction in drawing, pianoforte and European languages. Such accomplishments might serve as a passport to a happy married life for the upper-class white girls, but Thomas Crosby's concern for his native pupils was to teach them the skills to survive on their own and to be independent. "The most trying part of our work is to see the people sell their daughters . . . for the basest of purposes. There are villages where scarcely a young woman can be found."[107] As a result instruction at the Crosby Home stressed baking and sewing, and how to cull from the rocky soil a sufficient return of vegetables and berries to maintain life for a family through a Canadian winter. One of the school's boasts was that every graduate "was an expert in bread and bun making."[108]

Some of the students who came to the Crosby Home were orphans, but others came to escape being sold into prostitution, many as young as eleven or twelve years of age. Two of the early residents had been rescued by the Crosbys from a sacrificial devil's dance. They had been tied to a stake in the centre of a clearing while a band of male dancers had slashed at them with spears and knives cutting off pieces of flesh. Had the Crosbys not intervened the dance would have continued until both girls were dead.

Stories of boys running away from the Residential Schools are common, but no girl ever ran away from the Crosby Home. Historian Helen Meilleur describes the pupils sitting in church each Sunday morning motionless as statues in their navy tunics and wide-brimmed Eaton-catalogue hats while behind them a row of admiring men argued about which girl they intended to "catch" after their graduation. The girls smugly ignored them, knowing that with their new skills and newfound self-confidence they could do the choosing.[109]

Several other schools for native girls were started following the example of the Crosby Home, and together they provided a haven for scores of girls, but the number helped was only a fraction of those who needed it.

Then in the mid-1880s a new school for girls was established in Yale. The history of this school falls outside the time-frame of this study, but it is too unique to ignore, for this school was for both Indian girls and white girls.

Called All Hallows in the West, the school was brought into being by the efforts of the Right Reverend Acton Windeyer Sillitoe, Anglican Bishop of a new western Diocese, the Diocese of New Westminster.

Sillitoe insisted that it was not enough to have one or two elite schools for the daughters of the wealthy, and the occasional school like the Crosby Home as a refuge for the Indian children. He insisted that every girl had the right to be educated. Accordingly, when financial restrictions forced him to cancel his original plans to build two separate schools, one for white children and one for Indian pupils, he decided to build just one, a boarding school, which would provide under one roof identical educational opportunities for everyone.

He secured a small financial grant from one of the English missionary societies, then appealed to All Hallows School, Ditchingham, England, to send out several of their Order to start his school in the Canadian west.

Three Sisters of All Hallows, Ditchingham, set sail for the Canadian west—gentle, artistic Sister Althea who spent her leisure moments sketching the colourful wildflowers and the rocky wilderness terrain; motherly Sister Elizabeth Ann whose major concern was the purchase of a cow so the children would have fresh milk, then made a pet of the animal; and Sister Superior Amy, a princess in her Madrid homeland, but so nervous and high strung that a fourth Sister had to be sent out a short time later to assist with her duties.

The Sisters arrived in October, just as the Canadian winter was starting, to discover that the funds Sillitoe had been counting on were not forthcoming. Accordingly they took up residence in a room in a small section of the basement of the missionary house, took in washing to make money for their living, and settled for the time on running a "day school" where there would be a minimum of expense. Things went reasonably well for the winter, but when spring came attendance dropped sharply, as the pupils of the Sisters' day school together with their families moved with the game.

It was obvious that the only way in which a school for native pupils could be effective was for it to be a boarding school. Accordingly in 1885 Sillitoe purchased "Brookside," the large, rambling, white wood building at Yale that had been the home of CPR chief railroad contractor Andrew Onderdonk. It was well suited for a schoolhouse, for the rooms were large and airy, many had balconies, and the grounds were spacious. There was even a barn that Sillitoe converted into a chapel. To assist in financing the institution it was agreed that each white pupil would be billed fifteen dollars a month "plus additional charges for such extras as music and art,"[110] while the native students would help finance their education by performing gardening and household chores.

The only differences in the curriculum for white and non-white pupils was that while the white girls were studying music, drawing and foreign languages the Indian girls were learning "household chores and gardening."

There was also a difference in scheduling. Each morning the native girls arose an hour earlier than the white girls and used that hour to do general housekeeping chores. At mid-morning they set the tables for lunch while their white classmates were at recess. And during the hour before dinner while the white girls rested and changed their dresses, the Indian pupils prepared the vegetables and set the tables.

All the students, both native and "Canadian" as the white girls were called, studied the same subjects, sat together during classes and at mealtimes, and joined in the same social activities. Three years after the school was started Bishop Sillitoe reported that no prejudice of any kind was evident. More important, during the first ten years of the school's operation the annual lists of academic proficiency awards contained just as many Indian names as "Canadian" ones.

But inevitably discontent started to build. The parents of the white pupils, aggravated perhaps by the knowledge that they had to pay for their daughters' education while the native parents did not, demanded segregation within the school. They asked that partitions be erected in the classrooms, and that direct communication between white and non-white children be forbidden. Should they happen to meet, no sign of recognition was to be given, not even a nod or a smile. Even in the chapel on Sundays the Canadian girls in their white veils, fancy dresses and gloves sat on the opposite side of the chancel from the native girls in their red caps and pinafores, and each group was forbidden even to glance at the other.

The first Christmas after these new rules had been enforced two "Canadian" girls for some reason were unable to go home for the holidays. The Indian girls always spent Christmas at the school, for transportation to where their families might be spending the winter was difficult to arrange. As a result Christmas celebrations were always planned for them, but no one expected any white pupils to be still in residence so nothing was planned for them. That Christmas one of the white girls wrote home:

> At midnight there was a celebration of Holy Communion in the school chapel to which all the Indian children went, with about sixty visiting family members, but we were not allowed to go. From our dormitory we tried to listen to the singing.[111]

Two days later a big party was held around what was referred to as the Indian Christmas tree, but the two white girls were not allowed to go to that either.

Regrettably, the Residential School system established by the early missionaries and continued for more than half a century was directly responsible for alienating young native children from their language and their culture, and for destroying their pride in their heritage. Much of the criticism being levelled today against the Residential Schools for the injustices inflicted on native students is justified. Not only did many students suffer physical and mental abuse, the Residential School system set in motion among the entire native population a feeling of cultural inferiority that is only now beginning to be reversed. But in defence it must be stated that the original intention of the missionaries was to help, not to hurt. Faced with the problem of an itinerant people and a diversity of language that made communication impossible, the Residential School system seemed a logical solution.

It should also be noted that sociologists agree had it not been for the Residential Schools, where pupils were taught hygiene and health-care, the small-pox epidemic of 1862 which killed one-third of the native population west of the Rockies might have killed even more.

Also, there is a bright note. Over the past few years educators, government officials and the general public have begun to recognize and take responsibility for the damage that was done. They have started to take active steps to reverse it. Schools in various centres throughout the province are offering classes in native languages and in native culture. Schools in Lytton and Ashcroft have conducted classes in the Cree language. In Hazelton the Carrier language is being taught. Other Indian languages are being taught in Bella Coola, in the Nishga School District which includes the Nass Valley, in the city of Victoria, and at several locations in the Okanagan.

Chapter 7

METLAKATLA:
UTOPIA OR DICTATORSHIP

URING THIS TIME when the Men of God were actively taking the lead in developing educational institutions, and when their presence in the gold centres was starting to
influence life-styles and values, one of their number was responsible for
innovative leadership in another area. The man was William Duncan. His
accomplishment was the controversial Tsimshian settlement of Metlakatla.

Debate about Metlakatla is still continuing. For the more than 1500
Tsimshian who moved there with Duncan it offered a chance to learn and
grow and prosper. Even the Men of God who opposed it agreed that
Duncan had achieved amazing results. It existed for only two-dozen years,
but during that two-dozen years it effectively demonstrated the importance
of instilling in people a sense of self-worth, a sense of challenge, and an
opportunity for self-determination. Had Metlakatla been allowed to continue beyond its short life span, its example might have softened the tone of
subsequent government-native relations.

†

Metlakatla was established in 1862 by William Duncan, a lay catechist
trained by the Church Missionary Society in London. Metlakatla was built
sixteen miles northwest of Fort Simpson on the Pacific coast, on two acres
of land that had been donated to Duncan for the project by the Tsimshian
people.

"A notable achievement" the British parliament enthused when Metlakatla was at its height, and in many ways it was a notable achievement. "A
Canadian Utopia" said others. It was this too, though perhaps not quite in

the way the applauders meant. Rather it was "utopia" in the sense Sir Thomas More intended when in 1516 he coined the word for his romance: a visionary, impractical "nowhere."[112]

Duncan was not an ordained minister. He was a "catechist" prepared for missionary service by a period of training at one of the Missionary training schools run by the Church Missionary Society. This was standard procedure during the nineteenth century for men eager to offer themselves for such service. Britain had several Missionary schools, and none of them lacked for students.

The school Duncan attended was Highbury, but it would not have mattered if he had gone to Islington or to any one of the others. The training he received would have been the same, for all followed the same basic pattern. The standards were established by the Reverend Henry Venn, Executive Secretary of the Church Missionary Society.

Venn was convinced that religion had to grow from within a community, not be imposed by some outsider. He insisted that the chief task of a missionary should be to find and train local individuals to be ministers among their own people. The Missionary schools agreed. Accordingly, they developed a teaching program that did not centre around teaching philosophic thought or basic religious doctrine. It concentrated instead on teaching the student missionaries the principles of being effective teachers.

†

William Duncan first arrived in the Canadian far west in 1857, having come straight from the Church Missionary Society training centre at Highbury. His destination was Fort Simpson, with orders to start a mission there for the Tsimshian people. He approached the task with the dogmatic, single-minded determination that characterized all his activities.

Duncan was the only son of lower-class working parents and had been brought up in a small Yorkshire village near the town of Beverley. He was withdrawn, introverted and intensely ambitious. He was self-conscious about his humble beginnings and determined to better himself.

His first ambition was to become a success in business. His guide was a popular nineteenth-century lexicon called *The Young Man's Own Book* which was filled with pithy advice: "Time must be used to the fullest . . . Lying late in bed is an intemperance . . . Success depends on having fixed principles . . . To have a good memory you must be temperate in eating and drinking and sleeping."[113]

He made lengthy lists of "great lessons I have yet to learn," and wrote daily in his personal journal about his shortcomings.

His efforts at self-improvement were successful. He got a job in a wholesale tannery. At first it was a menial one but within a short time he was promoted to the position of traveller.

> Travelling threw me among a class of society which were above what I had been used to, among a class of men far my superiors in education, rank and abilities. I used to feel my heart overflow with gratitude for God's wonderful love in thus elevating me from the dunghill.[114]

Duncan was delighted with how things were going and impatient for more promotion so he could climb higher on the social scale. But this was difficult in nineteenth-century England where social position was primarily determined by birth.

That's when Duncan decided to abandon business and volunteer for missionary service, for that was the one way men of meagre education and lower-class parentage could win acceptance into higher levels of society.

He discussed the matter with his clergyman. Shortly afterward, on his minister's recommendation, the Church Missionary Society approached Duncan and invited him to consider the possibility of training for missionary work. Duncan readily agreed. At age twenty-two he left his selling post at the tannery and entered Highbury College.

The training school was a disappointment. Duncan had expected his fellow students would be upper-class, well-educated people, the group he longed to join, but they were men much like himself. His private journal admits:

> The students are not good enough, rich enough, polite enough, or intellectual enough for my pride. They do not reverence me as I have been reverenced at home. My dignity is wounded at finding myself lowered in circumstances and in class of acquaintance.[115]

Duncan's training in a missionary college rather than in a proper theological school is significant as events turned out. The fact that he was not an ordained cleric was a constant source of controversy between Duncan and Bishop George Hills and precipitated the major clash that destroyed Metlakatla. It was significant for another reason as well. Though perhaps it was not intentional, the training Duncan received at Highbury subtly instilled into the student missionaries the belief that people who had not been exposed to religion were inevitably lawless and immoral. It also instilled the belief that the unconverted could not be anything but unhappy and suffering. As a result Duncan arrived in the far west expecting that the native people were unhappy in their unconverted state and eagerly waiting to be converted not only to Christianity but also to European life-styles and values. This assumption on Duncan's part had a significant impact on his subsequent actions at Metlakatla.

Duncan was a complex figure. His personal strengths and weaknesses played a large part in the escalation of the drama that unfolded. In addition to his single-mindedness, his pride, his determination and his ambition, Duncan was also stubborn and intolerant.

This was apparent during Duncan's journey westward on Captain Prevost's vessel, HMS *Satellite.* Duncan had been assigned to a bunk in the engineers' quarters. However, the language used by some of the men, particularly the 2nd engineer, was considered by Duncan to be blasphemous so he complained to the captain. Prevost moved him to the gunners' quarters. Here the situation was no better, in fact it was worse, for news of Duncan's criticism of the engineers had spread throughout the ship and the gunners now went out of their way to annoy him. Accordingly Duncan got a large supply of rusks from the galley and moved into a small dinghy hanging from the davits at the stern of the ship. Despite the urgings of the captain it was not until almost the end of the journey that Duncan finally agreed to abandon his splendid isolation and move into the officers' quarters.[116]

Despite his shortcomings, however, Duncan was a remarkable man. He was a competent schoolteacher, a proficient musician, self-motivated to the point of being fanatical, and despite a limited education, highly intelligent. Within a matter of months of his arrival in Fort Simpson he had mastered the Tsimshian language and could converse easily with the native people. He was also innovative. Seeing the high incidence of illness among the Indians at Fort Simpson, and attributing it to their continually having their feet wet, he invented a wooden sole for their moccasins and taught them how to sew it in place.

One of Duncan's greatest gifts was his astuteness. He had initially been sent to work at Fort Simpson, which was agreed by everyone to be the best location for a mission in that area, but within weeks Duncan knew it was the worst possible choice. All nine Tsimshian tribes were settled around the Hudson's Bay fort there vying with each other for business. With the declining fur trade rivalry was intense. Also Fort Simpson was the centre of the liquor trade. Admittedly the Hudson's Bay traders were complying with Company regulations and refusing to sell liquor to the Indians, but the Americans just a short canoe trip down the coast were not so altruistic. An early Hudson's Bay journal describes the scene at Fort Simpson on the return of one of these canoes:

Nearly every one in camp is drunk—say about 500. Men, women and children. The Americans are the sole cause of this as our Indians obtained all the rum from Washington territory. Anything for the eternal dollar.[117]

Duncan was convinced a mission could never flourish anywhere near Fort Simpson. Not only was the liquor trade a major problem, its purchase was often financed by prostitution. Slavery, too, was still in practice. Not only were war hostages often kept as slaves, but in some cases whole nations were subjected to "servant" status by more powerful ones. On occasion a man might wipe out a slight or an insult by demanding the sacrifice of a slave belonging to the man who had offended him. Though the practice was not common there were instances where a major house in a settlement was erected with its central posts planted on the bodies of buried slaves.

In some areas cannibalism was still in evidence. One of Duncan's first experiences after arriving in the west in 1858 was watching a group of Tsimshian hunters kill and eat a slave girl.

Duncan was convinced that it would be almost impossible to teach Christian principles in such an atmosphere, so in 1862, five years after his arrival in western Canada, he took a small body of about sixty Tsimshian followers, left Fort Simpson, moved some sixteen miles farther up the coast to where a group of ten Tsimshian were already living, and established a Christian missionary settlement which he named Metlakatla.

Within months the seventy followers had swelled to five hundred. Within a year the population of Metlakatla numbered close to a thousand. Within a few more years it had almost doubled again.

Part of the reason for this growth was the steadily worsening situation that was developing at Fort Simpson. Discord and rivalry between the nine Tsimshian tribes camping in the area had escalated to the point where it was threatening to destroy tribal life. A second reason was the spreading smallpox epidemic. During the summer of 1862, the disease swept through many west coast communities. According to historian Peter Murray, 500 deaths were reported in Fort Simpson alone. Metlakatla did not escape. But thanks to Duncan's prompt action in acquiring vaccine from Victoria and inoculating the entire population, then insisting on proper treatment for the sick, only five smallpox deaths were reported in Metlakatla.[118] In the eyes of many Tsimshian, Duncan's relatively isolated community seemed to offer both security and safety.

Another factor contributing to the rapid growth of Metlakatla was Duncan's own personality. Not only had he won the respect of the

Tsimshian by learning their language, but he possessed those qualities they valued in themselves. He was as serious, patient, determined and unemotional as any Tsimshian. In addition he realized the importance of providing firm rules of conduct for an unsophisticated people.

His first step after establishing his missionary community was to draw up a fifteen-point code of behaviour for all residents. Included on the list was the prohibition of alcohol within the colony, the insistence that everyone must maintain a tidy house and a productive garden, the rule that every child must attend school, and the insistence that every resident must attend church services.[119] The rules were backed up with force. Duncan appointed officials from among the Tsimshian to make sure all the rules were obeyed and to report personally to him every day concerning any misdemeanours. Punishment was administered by Duncan, often with the lash. An item in his journal dated March 17, 1866 reads:

> I imprisoned Calvah the slave for a week and flogged him with sticks. After twenty lashes had been given I asked if he now felt his sin to smart. He said he did and thanked me for having had him punished.

Whippings were common treatment for school children too, particularly for the older boys who after working alongside the men all day, fell asleep during their obligatory school classes at night.

Duncan's most effective method for maintaining control was his practice of hoisting a black flag over the settlement when a misdemeanour had been committed. No mention was made of what the fault had been, but the wrongdoer was expected to come forward and accept his punishment. Until he did, the entire settlement suffered Duncan's displeasure. Peer pressure inevitably brought forth a flood of penitent wrongdoers, but Duncan never admitted which event had caused the raising of the flag. He dealt with every wrongdoer as if his was the major sin, in some cases banishing the guilty party from the settlement altogether.

The same strict discipline was evident in Duncan's administration of his Girls' Boarding Home. It was intended to train girls sixteen and over for marriage and motherhood but was run solely by Duncan. No female attendant or housekeeper or parent was allowed access. Duncan's word was law and his punishments went unchallenged.

> Last night I had to chastise Susan for inattention and gave all a very serious lecture on their careless, dirty, lazy habits. I had Margaret in prison (the cupboard under the stairs) for two days and nights for pilfering, and also added a severe beating.[120]

Having, with his rules of conduct, attained unquestioned authority over all aspects of Metlakatlan life, Duncan now turned his attention to making the community independent.

First he purchased a ship for $1500. Five hundred of this he borrowed from the government and later paid back; six hundred he put in himself; the remaining four hundred he raised by selling five- and ten-dollar shares in the vessel to the Metlakatlans. He named the ship *Kahah* meaning slave, and began selling soap and blankets made by his followers up and down the coast.

Immediately there was an outcry from the Hudson's Bay Company, for their own soap was a staple in fur-trade barter. One mink skin, valued at about a dollar, could be exchanged for a bar of Hudson's Bay soap about the size of a finger. Duncan offered a much larger bar for half the price. Before long the matter died a natural death, for Duncan's soap was made from the wrong kind of oil and no one wanted to buy more than one bar, but it served to draw the attention of the Hudson's Bay Company to what was happening in Metlakatla.

Duncan now began transporting goods other than those made by the Metlakatlans to centres up and down the coast. It was the commercial traders who protested this time, claiming that Duncan was trying to steal their business.

Next, Duncan turned his energies to building a sawmill and training his followers in all aspects of lumber preparation. Soon they had produced enough wood to reconstruct every building in the settlement and build an 800-seat Gothic cathedral. With the needs of their own community met, they then started selling lumber to surrounding communities.

Profits began to mount.

Duncan now established a store at Metlakatla, and included in it a "bank." Instead of paying his shareholders their dividends in cash, he gave them "bank accounts" which listed their earnings.

Finally, established church leaders began to be concerned. This was supposedly a religious settlement. They began to fear that making money might become more important to Duncan and his followers than worshipping God. Duncan, however, justified his actions with the argument that these commercial ventures were at the heart of his community's religious life, for only the self-reliant and the hard-working could be worthy followers of God.

Unquestionably, Metlakatla was a noteworthy accomplishment. It seemed to have escaped all the pitfalls that threatened other missionary settlements. Alcohol, for example, the curse of the west coast, was non-existent in Metlakatla. So was prostitution. Where other missionaries were struggling to find places to hold services and ways to attract worshippers, Metlakatla build a Gothic cathedral that seated 800 and filled it for every service. While other missions struggled to secure sufficient funds to feed and care for the needy, every citizen at Metlakatla was banking the dividends from a succession of community-run commercial operations.

Nor could Duncan be faulted on the grounds that he asked too much of his followers. He demanded the same hard work and determination from himself as he did from them. He utilized every moment, a habit, perhaps, gleaned from his *Young Man's Own Book*. He refused to let even ill-health serve as an excuse for idleness. Hills refers several times in his journal to Duncan's ill-health, and William Henry Collison reported to the Columbia Mission in 1879 ". . . my fellow missioner William Duncan had completely broken down in health." Historian Jean Usher suggests that Duncan probably suffered from tuberculosis during the whole time he was in Canada, but if this was true Duncan himself never mentioned it. He continued to push himself unstintingly, and largely due to his drive and energy Metlakatla continued to grow and prosper.

But criticism was beginning to build concerning the settlement, and one of the most outspoken critics was Bishop George Hills. At the outset Hills had praised Duncan's work, sending glowing reports back to the Columbia Mission, but gradually Hills's opinion changed. He began openly criticizing Duncan and Metlakatla.

For the first time the Church Missionary Society took a close look at Duncan's settlement. On the surface things appeared to be satisfactory, but the potential was there for serious mismanagement, for Duncan had unlimited power. In addition to being missionary and schoolteacher, he had established himself as secretary of the settlement, treasurer, head physician, chief carpenter, chief builder, guardian of moral and social behaviour, administrator of the Girls' Home, marriage counsellor, and proxy parent to all the children. In addition he had been made an official magistrate by Governor James Douglas, which under colonial law empowered him to settle all local disputes and petty misdemeanours and exact whatever punishment he deemed suitable. It also gave him the authority to establish a small police force of local citizens who would take orders solely from him. He had even constructed a "lock-up" in which to restrain offenders.[121]

By the mid-1870s the Church Missionary Society decided they could no longer ignore the situation. Not only was criticism growing about Duncan's personal power, now there was some question about his professional limitations. Much was made of the fact that he had failed to translate the scriptures into Tsimshian, though he spoke the language fluently. Duncan argued that it was impossible to express abstract thought in an Indian language and there was some validity to this argument, but the CMS could not disregard the suspicion that Duncan might have feared that translating the scriptures would weaken his power over his followers. This suspicion was supported by the knowledge that in the late 1860s William Henry Lomas, an Anglican catechist at Quamichan on Vancouver Island, had successfully translated the Anglican Book of Common Prayer into the Quamichan language and the native people there were using it for services.

Other concerns now began to surface centring around the services themselves, particularly whether or not Holy Communion should be administered. Duncan insisted the administration of the bread and wine at Communion would only confuse his followers. He pointed out that he had only recently succeeded in turning them from their earlier belief that eating the flesh of an animal was the way to gain that animal's strengths.

More harmful, however, than disagreements on doctrine or philosophy, were the personal misunderstandings, jealousies and accusations. Tempers flared. Bishop Ridley, the newly consecrated bishop of a third western diocese of Caledonia, Bishop Hills, and the Church Missionary Society all united against Duncan.

The discord erupted into open confrontation. Duncan's followers were caught in the middle, forced to take sides. They started drifting away.

By this time Duncan was ill and discouraged. Accepting an offer from the United States government of a piece of land in Alaska, Duncan packed up his settlement and moved north. But the new settlement never equalled the old one in numbers or accomplishments.

There was yet another unfortunate fallout of the whole affair. The original Metlakatla had been built on native land given by the Tsimshian people to Duncan in 1862 in a formal ceremony. It was given to him for the express purpose of creating a religion-centred Tsimshian settlement. When the escalation of the dispute between Hills, Ridley and Duncan forced the settlement to move, the Tsimshian followers requested that their land be returned to the Tsimshian people to whom it belonged. The young and inexperienced government of British Columbia refused to listen. Instead they "gave" the land to the Church Missionary Society in Britain.

It was a significant first misstep in future land controversy.

But overall, the example of Metlakatla had a positive impact on thinking in this new region. Metlakatla proved the importance of providing every citizen in a community with a sense of purpose and self-worth, and with an opportunity for self-achievement. It also proved that people who have not had the opportunity of any formal education can still readily develop skills and excel in useful occupations if they are given the opportunity.

Chapter 8

WATCHDOGS

THE METLAKATLA ISSUE was not the only one to centre around the question of power. Preventing unrestricted power from falling into the hands of a few enterprising officials was a major problem facing the missionaries on the far-west frontier during their first years.

Three thousand miles of unsettled country and a ridge of relatively impassable mountains isolated this far-west region from any sources of authority in eastern Canada. Both Britain and eastern Canada had little choice but to let the fledgeling colonial government in Victoria run its own show. The early missionaries provided the only check-rein on those who would otherwise had been free to make decisions and plan policy without any supervision or criticism.

The first issue of dispute concerned the desire of Colonial Governor James Douglas to establish government control over the church.

It is interesting to note that the same man who in 1850 refused to take any part in helping Robert John Staines build a church at Fort Victoria, eight years later in July 1858 informed the Imperial Parliament over which he presided that it would hereafter be the government's responsibility to decide where in the new colony churches could be built. He selected parcels of land at various locations throughout the territory and designated them as "clergy reserves." Hereafter, he stated, the decision would rest with the government as to whether or not a church was needed in a particular area, and if so, where and when it could be built. To ensure government control, Douglas stipulated that the land in this "clergy reserve" would be allotted to churches free of charge.

Immediately the danger was apparent. Not only would the government have control over the numbers of churches built, it could also refuse land to specific denominations. In the words of historian Howay, "At the very threshold of our colonial existence we were threatened with the possibility of having a State Church."[122]

When in July 1858, Douglas announced this plan to control religion, the Columbia Mission had not even been founded. There were only half a dozen clergy in the entire Victoria area: Roman Catholic Bishop Modeste Demers, Father Rondeault and Father Donkele, who were concerned primarily with the needs of their own congregations; Hudson's Bay chaplain Edward Cridge, who was constrained from criticizing the government by his HBC employers; and Anglican missionary Burton Crickmer, who was working some distance away from the centre of government. As a result no protest was raised.

Secure in the belief that he was free to do as he chose, Douglas proceeded to step two. In December 1858, six months after his initial announcement, he selected a site at Langley where he announced the first government-designated church and rectory would be built. The construction would be financed by the sale of crown lands in that district.

There was still no real protest, but there was at last some reaction. Victoria *Daily Colonist* editor William Alexander Smith, soon to rename himself Amor De Cosmos and subsequently to become provincial premier, wrote an editorial alerting the public to the danger of Douglas's plan. The editorial caused only minor repercussions, but those repercussions were enough to delay things for a short time, and that was all that was necessary. For in August 1859 Congregationalist minister William F. Clarke arrived in Victoria.

Immediately Clarke endorsed De Cosmos's warning, using the *Daily Colonist* as the vehicle for his opinion. Together with De Cosmos, Clarke succeeded in arousing sufficient public concern that Douglas was forced to back down. First he agreed to delay his plans for building a church in Langley until the matter could be more fully discussed. Then he capitulated entirely, and announced publicly that he would cancel his plan for a government-controlled "clergy reserve" and leave the building of churches to the clergy whose business it was.

However, though Governor Douglas may have lost a skirmish, he had not abandoned the war. He was still determined to exert as much government control as possible over everyone in the new colony, including the clergy. He saw a way to do this through Edward Cridge, the clergyman who had come to the area as the third Hudson's Bay Company chaplain.

Originally this whole new western region was administered by the Hudson's Bay Company. An agreement had been signed between the colonial government and the Hudson's Bay Company granting the Hudson's Bay Company full and absolute authority to open up and govern the new colony. Accordingly when Cridge was brought to Vancouver in April 1855 to be the third Hudson's Bay chaplain, he came as an employee of the Hudson's Bay Company. He came on a five-year contract, to be renewed, if the HBC decided to do so, in April 1860. The terms of his contract stipulated that "he should be provided with a parsonage and glebe of one hundred acres, of which thirty acres should be cleared and put in a cultivatible state, and that three-fourths of his stipend should be chargeable to and payable out of colonial funds."[123] This amounted to three hundred pounds per annum, paid from a trust fund of the Colony administered by Governor Douglas, and derived from the sale of land and other resources, chiefly Nanaimo coal.

In 1859, however, when Cridge's contract with the Hudson's Bay Company still had a year to run, the contract between the Colonial Office and the Hudson's Bay Company expired. No longer did the Hudson's Bay Company have "full and absolute authority" over the new colony. Instead the far-west wilderness had become an independent colony, about to be administered by its own civic government.

What caused the confusion was that this did not mean a change of leadership. For some years now James Douglas had served in two capacities, both as an official of the colonial government and as an employee of the Hudson's Bay Company. Accordingly he continued to be Governor of the new colony. And when at the end of that same year Cridge's five-year contract with the Hudson's Bay Company expired, Douglas in his dual capacity as Governor and Hudson's Bay Company official, claimed the authority to renew it. This meant in essence that the government was "hiring" a clergyman. Not only that, the government was "giving" that clergyman his church property and buildings with the stipulation that the "gift" would be reconsidered for renewal every five years.

In January 1860, just weeks after this issue surfaced, Bishop George Hills arrived in Victoria. He lost no time in reacting to the situation. Not only was he appalled that any civic official, governor or otherwise, should claim authority to hire or fire an ordained clergyman, he was even more incensed at the government's intention to "give" that clergyman his church buildings and a parcel of land. In his opinion this was one more dangerous offshoot of the "state-controlled church" issue that Clarke and De Cosmos thought they had solved a few months earlier. What clergyman "given" a generous parcel of land by the government, then forced to apply for the renewal of that "gift" at five-year intervals, is going to be in a position of strength to speak out against any questionable actions which that government might decide to take?

Hills insisted on an immediate meeting with Governor Douglas.

It took several meetings, but at last Hills succeeded in convincing Douglas to reduce the size of his "gift" from one hundred acres down to just thirty acres, and then to transfer ownership of the property out of Cridge's hands entirely and put it under the control of a body of church trustees. The argument Hills used centred around the insistence by Cridge that the hundred-acre holding belonged to him, personally, and on his death would remain the property of his family. Should this happen, Hills pointed out, "it would be an injury to the Church and to the succeeding Minister." He went on to add, "It would, moreover, stop efforts to raise an income now, supposing such a measure as pledging the land could be carried out."[124]

Douglas recognized the sense in Hills's argument.

The Anglican bishop then set to work to convince the Governor that Cridge (and all other clergy coming into the area) must be licensed under an episcopal licence signed by the Bishop, and that episcopal authority must supersede and permanently replace any civil contract between Cridge and the colonial government.

This time perhaps the personality of Cridge himself may have helped convince Douglas to accede to Hills's request. Cridge had been in the area since 1855 and was well known to Douglas. The Anglican cleric was extremely astute. He had distinguished himself at Cambridge with an outstanding academic record — far more outstanding than Hills's. Rather than being bound by convention as Hills was, Cridge was an admitted Evangelical. He was also somewhat of a radical. Perhaps Douglas envisaged constant confrontation between himself and Cridge, and decided it would be to his advantage to let Hills take over the responsibility for keeping the free-thinking Cridge in line. In any case, whatever the reason, he agreed to Hills's request.

It was a significant victory. It established the future of church independence in the province. However, it was won at the cost of damaged relations between Hills and his senior clergyman.

"He thinks he is ill used," Hills noted in his journal. It was an understatement. Cridge probably had cause to feel ill used. He had assumed that his ownership of the hundred-acre holding would provide his family with some security and a place to live after his death. Now this security had been taken away. Accordingly he appealed to the Bishop for some kind of compensation, but Hills refused even to discuss the matter.

†

Douglas, however, had not abandoned his campaign to gain state control over the church. He was just getting started. In mid-March, 1860, he summoned Hills to another meeting, this time to show him a copy of an official dispatch he had just issued to the government. It announced the establishment of hundred-acre grants of land to all four major denominations in any area where the population justified the building of a church.

Hills was furious, for Douglas had been careful to send out the dispatch before notifying Hills about it. There was now nothing Hills could do to stop it. In his journal notes regarding the meeting Hills digresses completely from the point at issue and expounds instead on the Governor's personal failings. First he belittles him for being so out of date that he does not even know the Methodists are no longer called "Episcopal Methodists." Next he suggests that Douglas should not be above listening to other people's opinions, for he is far from infallible, as had been proved by his insistence that New Westminster should be the capital of the new colony instead of Langley. He then castigates Douglas for being dictatorial, secretive in his dealings with other people, for considering everyone else to be his inferior, and for being vain and arrogant.[125]

It was not the first time Hills's annoyance over Douglas's high-handed actions was evident, nor was it his first reference to his determination to keep the government from interfering in church affairs. In a letter to the Missionary Society in London as early as March 1860 Hills wrote,

> When I arrived I found the papers full of warfare about the attempt to have a state church. . . . In my first sermon I proclaimed for liberty and told the people that upon them rested the burden . . . that I did not dream of resting upon the state.

That same fall of 1860 in a pastoral address to his clergy and people, Hills stated, "From the State we seek no exclusive privilege—we ask only for liberty, a fair field, and no favour."[126]

However, Hills's determination to escape government interference was not universally shared. Even the Columbia Mission had mixed feelings. James Douglas's offer to give the various churches free grants of land was discussed in London at the annual meeting of the Columbia Mission, in November 1860.

"In saying that we must depend upon the voluntary system [of financial support] and not upon the system of state endowment, we cannot conceal from ourselves the difficulties . . . difficulties which it would be folly to shut our eyes to at the present time," commented Chichester Fortesque.[127]

During the summer of 1861 the missionaries at two small communities started plans for building churches. One of these communities was Lillooet, the other was Port Douglas, the southern terminus of a new road through the mountain area north of Yale which had been authorized by Governor James Douglas and named in his honour.

When the residents of each of these small communities expressed an interest in erecting some sort of church building and started making plans for how this could be accomplished, Douglas immediately authorized the colonial government to provide financial grants to finance the cost of constructing a church in each place.

Hills's reaction was equally immediate and unequivocal. "I have this day taken an important step," he notes in his journal. "I trust I have been right. The Governor had lately made two grants toward the churches we are building in Douglas and Lillooet. I have written to the Church Committees to suggest their refusal of those grants."

He wrote to the churches explaining the disadvantages of accepting such a grant. It could start charges of favouritism among the other churches, he explained, provide the tax-paying public with an excuse to demand money for other schemes, and cause contention within the congregation itself. Hills promised if the churches would refuse the government money, he would increase his diocesan grant to each of them.[128]

The congregation at Douglas agreed. On August 7, 1861, they passed a resolution stating "Since his Lordship the Bishop regards it unfavorable, the Grant shall be declined." The congregation at Lillooet found the money too attractive to refuse. However, several months later they changed their minds. They decided to pay back the government grant.

Hills could hardly wait to arrange a meeting with Governor Douglas to inform him of the matter, but his pleasure was somewhat spoiled. Almost before he had finished telling the Governor of the decision by the parishioners at Lillooet, the Governor informed him that the people of Port Douglas had also had a change of heart. Regretting their earlier refusal of the money, they had written to ask if they were still eligible to receive their grant.[129]

The question of government land grants was being met with mixed feelings in other areas as well. Methodists Arthur Browning and Ephriam

Evans showed no reluctance to accept a grant of land in Barkerville on which to erect their small log cabin church. Anglican Missionary John Sheepshanks, meanwhile, paid $450 for the same size lot in Richfield for his small church, then used it for services for less than a year.

Hills, however, believed his stand was right. "The day is coming when such grants will be utterly repudiated by the local legislature," he wrote in his journal, adding that such action could be taken at the whim of any government, and the church would have no rebuttal. "Such is the precedent in all other colonies."

At last, his continued opposition had its effect. The government discontinued its campaign to try to secure either influence or authority over church policy.

†

In some areas, however, where the church and the government met in head-to-head confrontation the church was not quite so courageous. Such was the case in the matter of the descriptive booklets to advertise the new colony.

A plan was evolved to print and distribute a number of descriptive booklets extolling the glories of the new colony, and to distribute them at the second Great Exhibition of London, scheduled for the summer of 1862. Submissions were invited. From the large number received, two were selected. One of these was written by the Reverend Lunden Brown, Anglican rector of Lillooet.

When the Great Exhibition opened, however, Brown's booklet was not available. Colonial Governor James Douglas had refused to allow it to be published unless Brown agreed to rewrite a specific passage.

Brown refused.

The passage in question read: "The backward state of the country, the bad condition of the roads that exist, the waste of revenue in the construction of roads now abandoned (because in districts not frequented) and the underdeveloped state of the agricultural resources are owing to the maladministration of the Government."[130]

For over a year Brown held firm to his refusal to rewrite this passage, but finally he capitulated. In September 1863 when the booklet at last appeared in print the passage read:

"The manner in which the Government is carried on and the laws administered gives general satisfaction. So long as the Colony progresses and its new necessities are met by new enactments, the colonists (with the exception of an influential clique at New Westminster) are satisfied; they have not the wish, and in the present circumstances they would not have the time, to legislate for themselves."[131]

For rewriting the booklet Brown received fifty pounds.

The Victoria *Colonist* lost no time in commenting, "Of the clergyman who for the paltry sum of fifty pounds was found willing to betray his country and sacrifice good conscience, we can hardly trust ourselves to write."[132]

The editor of the *Colonist* was not the only one to protest. So did all three judges who had chosen Brown's original essay, Archdeacon Wright, Henry Holbrook and W. E. Cormack. They demanded that the government publish the original unaltered manuscript, for that was the version they had chosen. But the government knew it had won and didn't deign to reply.

†

Another conflict between church and state was in no way minor, and this time the clergyman involved did not back down. The issue, referred to by some historians as "The Cottonwood Scandal," put on trial the basic integrity of the provincial justice system.

The clergyman who brought the matter to public notice and launched an attack against the law's most prestigious figure was Methodist minister Arthur Browning. The person Browning attacked was high-profile Provincial Court Judge Matthew Baillie Begbie. The issue was a court decision concerning a man named Dud Moreland. The details of Moreland's case are not important—it is the actions of Judge Begbie that are significant.

Dud Moreland and his partner, Cox, were American land speculators who had been drawn to the Cottonwood area between Quesnel and Richfield by rumours that the colonial goverment might be considering that land for a townsite. The arrival in Cottonwood of a government land official seemed proof that a townsite was being considered. Moreland and Cox had their eyes on a particular area which they wanted for their own financial speculation, so while the colonial government debated what it would do, Moreland applied for a Pre-emption Certificate.

It was refused on the grounds that Moreland and his partner had to first make certain improvements on the land in question, to the minimum value of ten shillings an acre.

According to historian David R. Williams, Moreland and his partner made some improvements, then applied again, this time providing evidence that they had done the necessary work.[133] Again their application was refused. The court ruled that Moreland and Cox had still not done sufficient work on the pre-emption. There is some suggestion that the decision might have been influenced at least in part by the fact that the colonial government had at last made up its mind about the townsite and saw the advantage in holding the whole area in reserve.

The significance of the case now emerges, for shortly after the court ruled to refuse Moreland's application for pre-emption, Judge Begbie reversed that decision. What changed his mind, according to Arthur Browning, was the gift by Dud Moreland to Judge Begbie of twenty acres of the land in question.

In November 1862, using only the initial A to identify himself, Browning wrote out all the details of the case and sent it to the *British Columbian*.

Editor John Robson had never been a fan of Begbie's. He was also enough of a newspaper man to recognize a good story. The fact that the letter bore only an initial as identification didn't bother him, for he knew the identity of the author, so he agreed to publish it in a prominent spot in his paper.

Begbie was incensed. Immediately he began proceedings against Robson. He had him summoned to court and demanded a public apology and a retraction.

According to historians G. P. V. and Helen B. Akrigg, Robson appropriated the protection afforded by Browning's pseudonym and asked how he could either apologize or retract when he didn't know the identity of the correspondent. He assured Begbie, however, that if at some future date it should turn out that the judge had indeed been falsely accused, he would then happily comply with both requests.

It was hardly an answer that would placate a furious official. Begbie fined Robson for contempt of court and had him put in jail. For the next five days Robson's newspaper published melodramatic and amusing letters from their editor in his "foulsome cell,"[134] where he claimed to be surrounded by "wild shrieks of a dying maniac on the one hand, and the clanking of the murderer's chains on the other." Then he must have decided he and Browning had made their point, for he requested to be taken before Judge Begbie, submitted a written apology, and was released.

By now, rumours were widespread about the possibility that Begbie might have accepted land as a bribe in return for changing the pre-emption ruling. Begbie himself claimed to have "bought" the land in question for ten shillings an acre. Moreland, trying to make things better, succeeded only in making them worse by writing a letter to the *Colonist* stating that he had "given" the land to Begbie. He added that he felt he had every right to do so once the pre-emption had been granted and the land was his.[135]

Browning sent one final follow-up letter to the newspaper, then let the matter drop.

The truth concerning the affair is still not clear. Historian David Williams's comment goes perhaps as far as it is possible to go: "Historians have long pondered the true nature of the Cottonwood affair and Begbie's part in it."[136]

The important thing, however, is that Browning achieved his purpose. He alerted a trusting and ingenuous public to the realization that legal officials, like everyone else, are potentially capable of succumbing to the lure of monetary gain and self-interest.

✝

One final conflict raged between church and state and again the role played by the missionaries was significant. It concerned the issue of Indian land title.

It is significant that the situation that exists in British Columbia concerning land ownership is different from that anywhere else in Canada. A contributing factor in this as in so many other issues is the relative isolation of the far-west region at the time when the first decisions concerning land title were being made. The combination of distance and mountains screened British Columbia so effectively from the notice of the authorities in the east that the colonial officials felt free to plot their own course.

In the rest of Canada it was acknowledged that the native people who were in possession of the land at the time of the white man's arrival could continue to claim ownership to it until a formal treaty was drawn up and signed by an official of the Canadian government and by the native chief whose people occupied the land in question. In British Columbia this was never accepted. From the outset the colonial government in British Columbia insisted that all land belonged to the crown. They offered no legal justification for this, nor did they offer any explanation why the situation in British Columbia should be different from the rest of Canada.

From the moment that the Hudson's Bay Company's authority over the far-west area expired in 1859 and the colonial government took over, relations between government and native Indians started to deteriorate. By 1871 when British Columbia entered Confederation the situation was serious. Within two years it was critical.

On November 2nd, 1874 the Federal Minister of the Interior in Ottawa sent an official letter to the Provincial Government in British Columbia stating:

> A cursory glance . . . is enough to show that the present state of the Indian land question in our territory west of the Rocky Mountains is most unsatisfactory. If there has not been an Indian war it is not because there has been no injustice to the Indians, but because the Indians have not been sufficiently united.

By this time there were approximately thirty thousand white settlers living in British Columbia and thirty thousand Indians. The land settlement awarded to the Indians by the B.C. Provincial Government was a total of twenty-one thousand acres out of a provincial total of two hundred and eighteen million acres—a ratio of approximately one to ten thousand.

The issue of Indian land title and the role the missionaries played falls outside the time frame of this study, but the impact of the missionaries in land title debate was significant. Repeatedly they championed the native people and spoke out against the injustices of the government.

The efficacy of the mediation provided by such individual clergy as Methodists Alfred Green and Thomas Crosby was proven in the mid-1880s when an angry government passed a ruling to forbid any further admission of clergy into land claim hearings.

†

During the years between 1836 and 1871 when the region west of the Rockies was changing from an untamed wilderness into a civilized, mature, law-abiding region, the Men of God played a significant role. They influenced every facet of life, political, social, educational, legal and moral. They helped shape the emerging character of Canada's far west.

Not everything they did was successful, but they provided much-needed leadership when there was no other source of guidance or direction. They promoted education. They brought stability to the gold fields. They served as a crucial brake on an inexperienced and often headstrong colonial government. They were also among the first to speak out on the confusing and complicated issue of land title.

Had the Men of God delayed their arrival until after this crucial period, the personality and character of the province of British Columbia might have been significantly different.

NOTES

CHAPTER ONE

1 G. Hollis Slater, *B.C. Historical Quarterly*, Vol. VI, No. 1, January 1942.

2 Merk, Frederick, (ed.), *Fur Trade and Empire: George Simpson's Journal.* Cambridge Mass. 1931. p. 106.

3 *Op. cit.*, p. 108.

4 Gray, W. H., *History of Oregon*, Harris & Holman, Portland, 1870, p. 162.

5 *Ibid.*

6 Beaver, Herbert, "Experiences of a Chaplain at Fort Vancouver," *Oregon Historical Quarterly*, Vol. 39, (1938), ed. R. C. Clarke.

7 Frank A. Peake, *The Anglican Church in British Columbia*, Mitchell Press, 1959.

8 *Ibid.*, p. 20.

9 Report of the Founding Meeting of the Columbia Mission, November 16, 1859. *Columbia Mission Report.* VST Archives, Vancouver.

10 *Ibid.*

11 Hills's Journal. VST Archives, Vancouver.

12 Sheepshanks, the Reverend John, *Bishop in the Rough.* Cited: Akrigg, *B.C. Chronicle*, p. 185.

13 Hills's Journal, VST Archives.

CHAPTER TWO

14 D'herbomez Correspondence, Archives, Deschatels, Ottawa.

15 Thomas Crosby, *David Sallosalton*, United Church Archives, VST.

16 Simpson's Letters to London, 1841.

17 Akrigg, Helen and G. V. P., *British Columbia Chronicle, 1847-1871*, Vancouver, Discovery Press, 1977.

18 Ellen Mackay, *Places of Worship*, Sono Nis Press, 1988.

19 Jean Murray Cole, *Exile in the Wilderness*, University of Washington Press, 1979.

20 Frederick Merk, *Fur Trade and Empire, George Simpson's Journals, 1824-1825*, Harvard University Press, 1932. Introduction p. xxxii.

21 *Ibid.*

22 W. Kaye Lamb, *McLoughlin's Fort Vancouver Letters, 1839-44*, Introduction, p. 23. Hudson's Bay Record Society, 1943.

23 W. Kaye Lamb, *McLoughlin's Letters, op. cit.*

24 *Op. cit.*, p. xxxvii.

25 *Ibid.*, p. xxxv.

26 *Ibid.*

27 *Ibid.*

28 Margaret Atwood, *Days of the Rebels*, Canada's Illustrated Heritage, McClelland & Stewart, 1977.

29 Merk, *Fur Trade and Empire, 1824, op. cit.*

30 *Ibid.*

31 Akrigg, Helen and G. P. V., *British Columbia Chronicle, 1847-71*, Vancouver Discovery Press, 1977. p. 296.

32 G. Hollis Slater, *B.C. Historical Quarterly*, Vol. VI, No. 1, January 1942. "New Light on Herbert Beaver."

33 Peake, Frank, *The Anglican Church in British Columbia*, p. 4.

34 Herbert Beaver, "Experiences as a Chaplain at Fort Vancouver, 1836-38," *Oregon Historical Quarterly*, Vol. 39, (1938), ed. R. C. Clarke.

35 *Ibid.*

36 *Ibid.*

37 Letter of Staines to the secretary of the Hudson's Bay Company, March 7, 1848. Cited in Slater.

38 Letter of Roderick Finlayson, cited G. Hollis Slater, *op. cit.*

39 G. Hollis Slater, *B.C. Historical Quarterly*, October 1950.

40 *Ibid.*

41 Letter from James Robert Anderson cited in Slater, *op. cit.*

42 G. Hollis Slater, *op. cit.*, p. 214.

CHAPTER THREE

43 *They Call me Father: Memoirs of Father Coccola*, ed. Margaret Whitehead. University of B.C. Press, 1988.

44 *Op. cit.*, p. 11.

45 Edna Healey, *Lady Unknown: The Life of Angela Burdett-Coutts*, London, 1982.

46 Hills's Journal, February 24, 1863, Archives of the Ecclesiastical Province of British Columbia.

47 Letter from Hills to Cridge dated September 1, 1860, citing and commenting on 62nd Canon of the Church of England. VST Archives.

48 Hills's Journal, January 24, 1861.

49 Bishop Hills's Journal, August 1861, p. 132.

50 *Columbia Mission Report*, Provincial Archives of the Ecclesiastical Province of British Columbia, Vancouver School of Theology.

51 Hills's Journal, 1865, p. 34.

CHAPTER FOUR

52 Howay and Scholefield, *British Columbia*, Vol. II, p. 10. S. J. Clarke Publishing, Vancouver.

53 Bishop Hills's Journal, VST Archives.

54 "Sketches of Missionary Life," 1862, from R. J. Dundas's Journal, printed by SPCK, London. VST Archives.

55 *Inland Sentinel*, 1871, Barkerville Museum Archives.

56 Personal letter T. R. Mitchell to his family in Victoria, October 1862. Barkerville Museum Archives.

57 A. G. Garrett, "Mission Work in the Gold Fields of Cariboo," 1865. VST Archives.

58 Hills's Journal, May 3, 1862. VST Archives.

59 D. W. Duthie, *Bishop in the Rough*, Smith, Elder and Company, London, 1909.

60 *Op. cit.*

61 *Columbia Mission Report*, 1864.

62 A. C. Garrett, "Mission Work in the Gold Fields of Cariboo," 1865. VST Archives.

63 *Ibid.*

64 W. Kaye Lamb, Introduction, *Letters to Simon Fraser, 1806-1808*. Pioneer Books, 1960, pp. 52-55. Provincial Archives of B.C.

65 Letter of R. W. Haggen to W. N. Draper, dated November 27, 1930. PABC, quoting remarks by original Barkerville pioneer Harry Jones, and Robert Stevenson, partner of Cariboo Cameron.

66 *Cariboo Sentinel*, June 11, 1868.

67 *Cariboo Sentinel,* July 11, 1868 and July 26, 1868.

68 Skipton, "Life of George Hills," unpublished manuscript, VST Archives.

69 *Columbia Mission Report,* 1868, p. 26. VST Archives.

70 *Op. cit.,* p. 27.

71 Vancouver School of Theology Archives.

72 *Cariboo Sentinel* editorial, January, 1869.

73 *Columbia Mission Report,* 1869.

74 *Columbia Mission Report,* 1870.

75 *Columbia Mission Report,* June, 1870.

76 Letter Reynard to Hills, May 1870. VST Archives.

77 *Columbia Mission Report,* June, 1870.

CHAPTER FIVE

78 Hammerton, James A., *Emigrant Gentlewomen,* Croom Helm Ltd., London, 1979.

79 Letter to *The Times,* publ. April 7, 1862, written by the Reverend John Garrett.

80 *Columbia Mission Report,* 1862, VST Archives.

81 *Ibid.,* p. 54.

82 *Ibid.*

83 Garrett, Letter to *The Times,* April 7, 1862. PABC.

84 *Ibid.*

85 Hansard Debates, 3rd Series, Vol. CVIII, London, February 15, 1850.

86 Hills's Journal, March 31st, 1863.

87 Whymper, Frederick, *Travel and Adventure in the Territory of Alaska,* Harper, New York, 1871.

88 Gould, Jan, *Women of British Columbia,* Hancock House, 1975, pp. 38-39.

89 Article by Edgar Fawcett in "Tynemouth" file, PABC.

90 Lugrin, Nancy de Bertrand, *The Pioneer Women of Vancouver Island,* Victoria, The Women's Canadian Club, 1928, p. 156.

91 Hills's Journal, October 4, 1862.

92 *The Colonist,* April 17, 1948

93 Information contained in a letter from Edward Cridge to James Douglas, July 14, 1863, PABC.

94 Lay, Jackie, "To Columbia on the *Tynemouth," In Her Own Right,* ed. Barbara Latham and Cathy Kess, Camosun College, 1980.

95 Gresko, Jacqueline, "Two Women on the Frontier," unpublished MS, Saskatoon, 1979, p. 22.

96 Lugrin, Nancy de Bertrand, *The Pioneer Women of Vancouver Island,* Victoria, The Women's Canadian Club, 1928.

CHAPTER SIX

97 Merk, *Fur Trade and Empire: George Simpson's Journals, 1824-25,* Harvard University Press, 1931, p. 135.

98 *Simpson's Letters to London,* ed. Glyndwr Williams, Hudson's Bay Record Society, Letter November 25, 1841, p. 84.

99 W. L. Morton, Address to the Historical Society of Trent University, *Historical Papers,* 1970, p. 46.

100 G. Hollis Slater, *B.C. Historical Quarterly,* October 1950, Vol. VI, No. 1. "Rev. Robert John Staines, Pioneer Priest, Pedagogue and Political Agitator."

101 *Columbia Mission Report,* 1860.

102 *Columbia Mission Report,* reprint of a letter dated September 17, 1868.

103 *Columbia Mission Report,* VST Archives.

104 Letter from George Hills to Angela Burdett-Coutts cited in the *Columbia Mission Report,* June 1860.

105 Isobel McFadden, "Living by Bells," Study Paper, United Church Archives, Vancouver, 1971.

[106] *Ibid.*

[107] Thomas Crosby, *Up and Down the Pacific Coast*, United Church Archives, Vancouver.

[108] Wesleyan Missionary Notices, 1869-78. United Church Archives, Vancouver.

[109] Helen Meilleur, *A Pour of Rain*, Victoria, Sono Nis Press, 1980.

[110] Jean Barman, "Separate and Unequal," B.C. Studies Conference, 1984, VST Archives.

[111] *Ibid.*

CHAPTER SEVEN

[112] Britannica World Language Dictionary, Gr. ou = not; topos = place.

[113] Jean Usher, *William Duncan of Metlakatla*, National Museum of Canada, Publication #5, Ottawa, 1974. p. 4.

[114] *Ibid.*, pp. 3-4. April 10, 1855. WD/C2154.

[115] *Ibid.*, p. 9. July 26, 1854.

[116] Akrigg, Helen and G. P. V., *B.C. Chronicle, 1847-1871*, Discovery Press, 1977, p. 264.

[117] Hudson's Bay Journal, Kamloops Museum Archives.

[118] Peter Murray, *The Devil and Mr. Duncan*, Sono Nis Press, Victoria, 1985.

[119] Welcome, Henry S., *The Story of Metlakatla*, Saxon & Co. London, 1887. p. 20.

[120] Duncan's Journal, November 19, 1865, WD/C2155. Cited by Usher, *op. cit.*, p. 83.

[121] Welcome, Henry S., *The Story of Metlatkatla*. Saxon & Co., London, 1887. Report from Colonel Vincent Colyer in his office as Special Commissioner.

CHAPTER EIGHT

[122] Howay & Scholefield, *British Columbia, op. cit.*, p. 616.

[123] *Ibid.*

[124] Hills's Journal, *op. cit.*, Wednesday, March 12, 1862.

[125] Hills's Journal, March 21, 1862, VST Archives.

[126] *Columbia Mission Report*, 1860, p. 43.

[127] *Ibid.*, p. 19.

[128] *Columbia Mission Report*, 1861.

[129] Hills's Journal, February 1862.

[130] Akrigg, Helen and G. P. V., *British Columbia Chronicle, 1847-1871*. Discovery Press, Vancouver, 1977, p. 280.

[131] *The British Columbian*, September 12, 1863, cited by Akrigg.

[132] Akrigg, *op. cit.*

[133] Williams, David, R., *The Man for a New Country*, Gray's Publishing, 1977.

[134] Akrigg, *op. cit.*

[135] Williams, David R., *The Man for a New Country*, Gray's Publishing, 1977. p. 194.

[136] Williams, David R., *op. cit.*, p. 196.

SELECTED BIBLIOGRAPHY

NEWSPAPERS AND PERIODICALS

British Colonist (Victoria).

British Columbian (New Westminster).

Cariboo Sentinel.

Church Missionary Intelligencer.

Columbia Mission Report, 1859 through 1880, VST Archives, Vancouver.

The Times (London).

Inland Sentinel.

The Press (Victoria).

The Times (London).

UNPUBLISHED SOURCES

Canons of the Church of England, VST Archives.

Cridge, the Reverend Edward. Personal correspondence.

PABC.

D'herbomez Correspondence, Archives, Deschatels, Ottawa.

Duncan, William—Journal, WD/C2155.

Gresko, Jacqueline, "Two Women on the Frontier," unpublished MS, Saskatoon, 1979.

Hills, Bishop George—Journals.

Hills, Bishop George—private correspondence, VST Archives.

Hudson's Bay Journal, Kamloops Museum Archives.

Letter of R. W. Haggen to W. N. Draper, dated November 27, 1930. PABC.

Letter T. R. Mitchell to his family in Victoria, October 1862. Barkerville Museum Archives.

McFadden, Isobel, "Living by Bells," Study Paper, United Church Archives, Vancouver, 1971.

Skipton, J. H. K., unpublished manuscript, "Life of George Hills."

"The Work of the Oblates in Cariboo," UBC Special Collections.

PUBLISHED SOURCES

Akrigg, Helen and G. V. P., *British Columbia Chronicle, 1847-1871,* Vancouver, Discovery Press, 1977.

Atwood, Margaret, *Days of the Rebels,* Canada's Illustrated Heritage, McClelland & Stewart, 1977.

Barman, Jean, "Separate and Unequal," B.C. Studies Conference, 1984.

Beaver, Herbert, "Experiences of a Chaplain at Fort Vancouver, 1836-38," *Oregon Historical Quarterly,* Vol. 39, (1938), ed. R. C. Clarke.

Begg, Alexander, *History of British Columbia from its Earliest Discovery to the Present Time,* Toronto, William Briggs, 1894.

Coccola, Father Nicolas, Memoirs, *They Call me Father,* ed. Margaret Whitehead. University of B.C. Press, 1988.

Cole, Jean Murray, *Exile in the Wilderness,* University of Washington Press. 1979.

Crosby, Thomas, *David Sallosalton, Young Missionary*, Methodist Church Missionary Society, 1914.

———, *Up and Down the Pacific Coast*, Methodist Church Missionary Society, 1914.

Dundas, The Rev. R. J. "Sketches of Missionary Life," London, SPCK, 1862.

Duthie, The Rev. D. W., *Bishop in the Rough*, Smith, Elder and Company, London, 1909.

Fawcett, Edgar, "Some Reminiscences of old Victoria," Toronto, William Briggs, 1912.

Fisher, Robin, *Contact and Conflict: Indian–European Relations in British Columbia, 1774-1890*. Vancouver, UBC Press, 1977.

Garrett, The Rev. A. G., "Mission Work in the Gold Fields of Cariboo," CMS 1865.

Gould, Jan, *Women of British Columbia*, Vancouver, Hancock House, 1975.

Gray, W. H., *History of Oregon*, Portland, Oregon, Harris & Holman, 1870.

Hammerton, James A., *Emigrant Gentlewomen*, London, Croom Helm Ltd., 1979.

Hansard Debates, 3rd Series, Vol. CVIII, London. February 15, 1850.

Healey, Edna, *Lady Unknown: The Life of Angela Burdett-Coutts*, London, Sidgewick and Jackson, 1978.

Howay, F. W. and Scholefield, E. O. S., *British Columbia, From the Earliest Times to the Present*, Vol. II, Vancouver, S. J. Clarke Publishing Co., 1914.

Lamb, W. Kaye, *McLoughlin's Fort Vancouver Letters, 1839-44*, Hudson's Bay Record Society, 1943.

———, *The Letters and Journals of Simon Fraser, 1806-1808*. Pioneer Books, Macmillan of Canada, 1960.

Lay, Jackie, "To Columbia on the Tynemouth," *In Her Own Right*, eds. Barbara Latham and Cathy Kess, Camosun College, 1980.

Lugrin, Nancy de Bertrand, *The Pioneer Women of Vancouver Island, 1843-1866*. Victoria, The Women's Canadian Club of Victoria, 1928.

Mackay, Ellen, *Places of Worship in the Cowichan and Chemanus Valleys*, Victoria, Sono Nis Press, 1988.

McFadden, Isobel, "Living by Bells," Study Paper, United Church Archives, Vancouver, 1971.

Meilleur, Helen, *A Pour of Rain*, Victoria, Sono Nis Press, 1980.

Merk, Frederick, ed. *Fur Trade and Empire, George Simpson's Journals, 1824-1825*, Cambridge Mass. Harvard University Historical Studies, 1931.

Morton, W. L., "Histriography of the Great West," Address to the Historical Society of Trent University, *Historical Papers*, Canadian Historical Association, 1970.

Ormsby, Margaret, A., *British Columbia, a History*, The Macmillan Co. of Canada, 1958.

Peake, Frank A., *The Anglican Church in British Columbia*, Vancouver, Mitchell Press, 1959.

Slater, G. Hollis, "New Light on Herbert Beaver." *B.C. Historical Quarterly*, Vol. VI, No. 1, January 1942.

———, "Rev. Robert John Staines, Pioneer Priest, Pedagogue and Political Agitator." *B.C. Historical Quarterly*, October 1950, Vol. 14, pp. 187-250.

Usher, Jean, *William Duncan of Metlakatla*, National Museum of Man, Publications in History, No. 5, Ottawa, 1974.

Welcome, Henry S., *The Story of Metlakatla*, London, Saxon & Co., 1887.

Williams, David R., *The Man for a New Country*, Gray's Publishing, 1977.

Williams, Glyndwr, ed. *Simpson's Letters to London*, Hudson's Bay Record Society, Letter, November 25, 1841, Glasgow University Press, 1973.

Whymper, Frederick, *Travel and Adventure in the Territory of Alaska*, London, W. Clawes & Sons, 1868; New York, Harper, 1871.

Yarmie, Andrew H., "Smallpox and the British Columbia Indians—Epidemic of 1862." *B.C. Library Association Quarterly*, 1968.

INDEX

Other Missionary History Titles published by Sono Nis Press

THE DEVIL AND MR. DUNCAN

A History of the Two Metlakatlas

by PETER MURRAY

WARRIORS OF THE NORTH PACIFIC

Missionary Accounts of the Northwest Coast, the Skeena and Stikine rivers and the Klondike 1829-1900

Edited and Annotated by CHARLES LILLARD

IN THE WAKE OF THE WAR CANOE

William Henry Collison's forty years of labour, peril and adventure amongst the Indian tribes of the Pacific coast and the Haida of the Queen Charlotte Islands

Edited and Annotated by CHARLES LILLARD

THE CARIBOO MISSION

A History of the Oblates

by MARGARET WHITEHEAD